BE JESUS
IN YOUR NEIGHBORHOOD

DEVELOPING A PRAYER, CARE, SHARE LIFESTYLE IN 30 DAYS

By Alvin VanderGriend

with Edith Bajema, John F. DeVries, and David J. Deters

PRAYERSHOP
PUBLISHING

Terre Haute, Indiana

PrayerShop Publishing is the publishing arm of the Church Prayer Leaders Network. The Church Prayer Leaders Network exists to equip and inspire local churches and their prayer leaders in their desire to disciple their people in prayer and to become a "house of prayer for all nations." Its online store, prayershop.org has more than 150 prayer resources available for purchase or download.

ISBN: 978-1-935012-29-0

2 3 4 5 | 2021 2020 2019

INTRODUCTION

This devotional can change your life!

How?

By getting you in the habit of consistently praying for the salvation of neighbors and co-workers . . . and putting God's heart of love into you so you will want to care for and share Christ with them. All of us know the importance of praying for our friends and family to come to a knowledge of Jesus Christ and give their lives to him. But it is hard both to be consistent and to know what to pray beyond "bless them, Lord."

As you individually, or with your group, pray through *Be Jesus in Your Neighborhood*, you will catch a passion for a concept called Prayer-Care-Share. This concept simply means that first we need to pray for lost people, then we need to show the love of Christ to them, and finally we will gain an opportunity to share Christ with them.

This devotional is set up simply. The first ten days teach you more about praying effectively. But as you pray, you will begin to experience God's heart for your neighbors and co-workers. The second ten days focus on caring for your neighbors—how to both pray for and spot opportunities to show the love of Christ to them. Finally, the last ten days develop within you a desire to share the love of Christ.

Each day has a Reflection and Action section and two areas to focus your prayers. You will notice, ironically, that while we are seeking to provide you with things to pray beyond "Lord, bless them," this booklet will teach you to B.L.E.S.S. them! We often use this acronym to shape the content of the prayer sections. It stands for:

B – Body (health)

L – Labor (work situations)

E – Emotional (mental health)

S – Social (relationships)

S – Spiritual (relationship with Jesus Christ)

We hope that as you read and pray through *Be Jesus in Your Neighborhood,* God will use this experience to change your life, that he will give you his passion and love for the people around you, and that you will become a believer who becomes Jesus to those next to you.

A Word about the Authors:

There are four contributors to this book.

The first ten devotions (Prayer) were written by Alvin VanderGriend, the author of the best-selling devotional, *Love to Pray*. These ten devotions also appear in that publication.

The second ten (Care) were written by one of three writers: Edith Bajema(EB), a freelance writer from Grand Rapids; John F. DeVries (JDV), retired director of Mission India; and Alvin VanderGriend (AVG). At the end of each devotional, you will see the initials of its author.

The third ten (Share) were all written by David J. Deters, the pastor of Alger Park Christian Reformed Church in Grand Rapids, Michigan.

Our prayer is that this devotional will forever change your life, as you learn to be Jesus in your neighborhood.

DAY 1

FRIENDSHIP WITH GOD

You have made known to me the path of life;
you will fill me with joy in your presence,
with eternal pleasures at your right hand. —PSALM 16:11

Human beings are created to live in fellowship with God. We are meant to have and to enjoy life in relationship with God. Without this relationship, we are like branches cut off from a tree, like toasters not plugged in.

Prayer is the way we get in touch with God and the way we keep in touch with him. I used to think of prayer as a spiritual exercise, a discipline that had to be worked at. Through the years, however, God has taught me to see it more and more as the talking part of a friendship. One of the early church fathers called it "keeping company with God." I like that!

Several years ago as I tried to define prayer, God led me through a series of steps. At first I thought of prayer simply as *talking with God.* Then, the idea of relationship emerged, and I began to see that prayer is the talking part of a *relationship* with God. Months later my definition changed again, and I began to understand that prayer is *the talking part of a love* relationship with God. But there was still more I had to learn. I came to see that prayer was the talking part of the *most important* love relationship in our lives. With that addition I thought that I finally had it, but some years later God added one more element. Then the definition, a definition that I still live with today, came out as: "prayer is the conversational part of the most important love relationship in our lives, *our love relationship with the Father, the Son and the Holy Spirit.*"

Sometimes people ask how much time they should try to spend in prayer each day. I used to suggest that twenty minutes of formal prayer a day was a minimum. I reinforced that by reminding them of the many things that need to be included in prayer, and then I added that twenty minutes a day was only about 2 percent of our waking hours each day.

Now when people ask about the time they should spend in prayer, I simply tell them they should spend enough time to build a good relationship. Considering that the relationship we are talking about is life's most important love relationship, that means plenty of time.

What does God do for those who relate to him in love? The psalmist put it well when he said, "You will fill me with joy in your presence, with eternal pleasures at your right hand."

What's the good of prayer? Just this! It helps us to grow into and live out of that most important of all love relationships. But, of course, it's only as good as we make it. So, what good are you making of it?

Reflect/Act

What can your prayer life tell you about your love relationship with God?

What more could you do to deepen your friendship with God?

Prayer Starters for Praying Psalm 16:11

- *Praise* God for his love and for his readiness to have a love relationship with you.
- *Ask* God to strengthen your prayer life and deepen your relationship with him.
- *Ask* God to fill you with joy in his presence and to give you eternal pleasures at his right hand.
- *Thank* God for his generosity in making these gifts available.

Pray a BLESSing on those who live or work near you:

- **Body (physical).** Pray that the Father who sends "every good and perfect gift . . . from above" (James 1:17) will meet their needs.
- **Labor (work).** Pray for diligence in work. "Lazy hands make a man poor, but diligent hands bring wealth" (Proverbs 10:4).
- **Emotional (inner life).** Pray that they may have the Holy Spirit and his fruit. "The fruit of the Spirit is love, joy, peace, patience, kindness, goodness, faithfulness, gentleness and self-control" (Galatians 5:22-23).
- **Social (relational).** Ask God to give them good friendships. "Pity the man who falls and has no one to help him up!" (Ecclesiastes 4:10).
- **Spiritual.** Pray that they will "receive forgiveness of sins and a place among those who are sanctified by faith in [Christ]" (Acts 26:18).

Pray also for specific needs you are aware of.

DAY 2

PRAYER STARTS WITH GOD

The Spirit helps us in our weakness. We do not know what we ought to pray for, but the Spirit himself intercedes for us with groans that words cannot express. And he who searches our hearts knows the mind of the Spirit, because the Spirit intercedes for the saints in accordance with God's will. —ROMANS 8:26-27

I want to share a radical thought. It has transformed my way of praying and my way of thinking about prayer.

For years I believed that my prayers started with me. I had to think them up. I had to get God's attention. Not surprisingly, with this frame of mind, prayer was often a chore.

I learned that I was wrong. Prayer doesn't start with us. *Prayer starts with God.* That's the radical idea that changed my prayer life. God is the initiator. He moves us to pray. He gives us prayer ideas. He holds out the promises we claim in prayer. When we pray, we are God's instruments.

God is at work in all our praying. He makes his will known to us so that we will ask for the very things he longs to give us. Out of love he burdens us to pray for others so that, in response to our intercession, he can pour out blessings on them.

And it's the Spirit, says Paul, who makes our prayer possible. We don't know what to pray, but we don't have to. The Spirit is there revealing God's will to us in the Scriptures and bringing God's prayer concerns to life within us. He is nudging us through circumstances and opening our eyes to the needs around us. He is searching our hearts and trying our ways so that he can bring us to true repentance. He is revealing the glory and the goodness of God so that our prayers will be filled with praise and thanks.

We can be confident that God will hear when we come to him. God answers every prayer that starts in heaven, every prayer born in our hearts by the Holy Spirit, every prayer based on a sure promise from his Word.

If prayer starts with God, then the first order of business as we learn to pray is to learn to listen to God's whispers, to tune our hearts to him, to respond to his promptings. Perhaps the first prayer of each day should be "Lord, teach me to pray. Help me to understand your purposes, to feel your burdens, to see what you see, to hear the groans you hear, so that my prayers may be pleasing to you and may accomplish your purposes."

How about starting right now: "Lord, teach me to pray today."

Reflect/Act

Is prayer a chore or a joy for you?

What more could you do to be sure that you truly know God's will when you pray?

Prayer Starters for Praying Romans 8:26-27
- *Praise* the Lord as the prayer-initiating, prayer-hearing God.
- *Ask* God to make prayer a joy in your life.
- *Thank* God for the privilege of knowing his thoughts and praying them back to him.

Pray a BLESSing on those who live or work near you:
- **Body.** Pray that the Father in heaven who "causes his sun to rise on the evil and the good, and sends rain on the righteous and the unrighteous," will bless them (Matthew 5:45).
- **Labor.** Pray that they may have employment and adequate compensation from it. "He who tends a fig tree will eat its fruit" (Proverbs 27:18).
- **Emotional.** Pray that they will take their cares, hurts, and disappointments to the Lord. "Cast all your anxiety on him because he cares for you" (1 Peter 5:7).
- **Social.** Pray for love, devotion, and sexual purity in marriages. "Marriage should be honored by all, and the marriage bed kept pure" (Hebrews 13:4).
- **Spiritual.** Pray that they will call on the name of the Lord and be saved (Acts 2:21).

Pray for specific needs you are aware of.

Let the Holy Spirit nudge you on how to pray for your neighbors or work associates.

DAY 3

CELEBRATING GOD THROUGH PRAYER

I will extol the Lord at all times;
his praise will always be on my lips.
My soul boasts in the Lord;
let the afflicted hear and rejoice.
Glorify the Lord with me;
let us exalt his name together. —PSALM 34:1-3

Everyone loves a good celebration. And life gives us plenty of opportunities to celebrate. We celebrate Christmas, the new year, birthdays, anniversaries, graduations, victories, and more. But there is no better reason to celebrate than God.

To celebrate means "to honor or praise publicly." God deserves honor and praise more than anyone or anything else. The great Scottish preacher Alexander Whyte used to counsel his hearers to "think magnificently of God." People who think magnificently of God, calling to mind his greatness and goodness, cannot help but celebrate God and declare his praise.

We live in a society that delights to celebrate worth. We exalt Super Bowl heroes, we gush over favorite movie stars, and we glory in our nation's victories. Not all of that is bad. But in the process of lifting up and extolling let's not forget the one who is the source of all good things.

To celebrate God means at least three things:

First, it means *recognizing God for who he is*. God's glory is his majestic splendor shining out so it can be seen and known. When we glorify God, we don't give him anything. We don't add luster to him. That's as impossible as it is to add splendor to a sunset by viewing it. But we can gaze in wonder at a sunset, and similarly we can behold in awe the beauty and glory of the Lord.

Second, it means *loving God for who he is*. This means laying aside our concerns, our demands, and our prayer lists to focus on God and to enjoy him. Nothing does more to quell pride, self-centeredness, and selfish desires than to focus beyond ourselves on God alone.

Third, celebrating God means *giving God the only thing we can offer him*—our loving, praising hearts. He already has everything else. He is totally self-sufficient and needs nothing from us. But God does ask us to give to him our hearts, our love, and our adoration. When we do, he is pleased and blessed.

Let's start today by thinking "magnificently of God." Everything else will follow.

Reflect/Act

How much do you enjoy God? Do you ever take personal time just to think about God and his goodness and to worship him?

Think of some specific ways that you can celebrate God today.

Prayer Starters for Praying Psalm 34:1-3
- *Praise* God by telling him five things you especially appreciate about him.
- *Ask* God to help you see his majestic splendor and to truly enjoy him and love him.
- *Thank* God for revealing his glory and for giving you reason to boast about him.

Pray a BLESSing on those who live or work near you:
- **Body.** Pray that, for all their needs, they may look to God, who is prepared to "give them their food at the proper time" (Psalm 145:15).
- **Labor.** Pray that they may keep their lives "free from the love of money and be content with what [they] have" (Hebrews 13:5).
- **Emotional.** Pray that they may have "the unfading beauty of a gentle and quiet spirit, which is of great worth in God's sight" (1 Peter 3:4).
- **Social.** Pray that they will "bear with each other and forgive whatever grievances [they] may have against one another" (Colossians 3:13).
- **Spiritual.** Pray that they may confess Jesus as Lord, believe God raised him from the dead, and be saved (Romans 10:9).

Pray for specific needs of these individuals for whom you are praying. Be open to impressions and burdens of the Holy Spirit and pray as he leads you.

DAY 4

PRAYING IN JESUS' NAME

Until now you have not asked for anything in my name. Ask and you will receive, and your joy will be complete. —JOHN 16:24

By offering to let us pray in his name, Jesus is offering an amazingly great privilege. It's as if he is giving us blank checks to be drawn on his account, knowing we will use them for his honor and his advantage.

Jesus is demonstrating great trust in us. He is trusting that his honor and his interests are safe in our hands. Consider what it would mean to place your estate in the hands of another person: your credit cards, your home, your investments, your automobiles, your responsibilities, everything. You'd pick that person very carefully, wouldn't you? You'd really be giving that person control over your life and your future.

That's essentially what Jesus did when he authorized us to use his name in prayer. He gave us authority over his accounts. He asked us to exercise control over his estate—the kingdom of God.

We exercise our authority by prayer. By prayer, we ask the Father for all we need in order to do the job. By prayer, we ask God to deal with demonic forces contrary to his will. By prayer, we direct God's grace and power to strategic locations where it is needed.

Three phrases in particular help us understand what it means to pray in Jesus' name. First, we are authorized to be Christ's representatives. When we come to the Father in Jesus' name, we come as those who are authorized to act in his place. We "represent" him. When we stand before the throne, the Father recognizes us as persons who stand in the place of his Son. That makes us acceptable.

Second, we come to God on the basis of Christ's merit. You and I have no claim on God, but Christ does. He merited the Father's favor by his perfect life and sacrifice. When we come in Jesus' name, we are identified with him. We come on the ground of his claim on the Father. Our access depends solely on what Jesus has done.

Try to imagine yourself coming to the Father on your own, apart from Christ. You are unauthorized to come, because you have no claim on God's favor. In fact, you have a huge debt with God because of your sins and you can expect nothing but God's blazing wrath. That's the opposite of coming in the name of Jesus.

Third, we come asking in accordance with Christ's will. We have the mind of Christ in us (1 Corinthians 2:16), so what we ask is what Jesus would ask. He is asking us to ask for him. We are able to ask what he would ask because our wills are in sync with his will.

The Father so loves the Son that when we introduce the Son's name in prayer, we have his ear, we have secured his willingness, and we have touched his heart.

Reflect/Act

Think about the responsibility you have for building some part of Christ's kingdom. What help do you need from the Lord to do this well?

What can you do to learn how to be more conscious of Jesus' will as you pray in his name?

Prayer Starters for Praying John 16:24

- *Praise* God for the gracious provision of his Son, Jesus Christ, as the One through whom you are able to approach the throne and receive a hearing from God.
- *Confess* any selfish praying that has not truly represented the mind of Christ and has not been in accord with his will.
- *Ask* for anything you need in order to accomplish God's will in your life and in your world.

Pray an expanded version of the Lord's Prayer (Matthew 6:9-13) for those who live or work near you:

- **God's Concerns.** Pray that they may know the Father who is in heaven, that their lives would glorify God, that his kingdom will be established in their homes and workplaces, and that they will desire to do his will as do the angels in heaven.
- **Human Concerns.** Pray that God will provide for their daily needs, forgive their sins, keep them from falling into temptation, and protect them from the devil's schemes.

DAY 5

GOD SEEKS INTERCESSORS

"I looked for a man among them who would build up the wall and stand before me in the gap on behalf of the land [of Israel] so I would not have to destroy it, but I found none. So I will pour out my wrath on them and consume them with my fiery anger, bringing down on their own heads all they have done, declares the Sovereign Lord."
—EZEKIEL 22:30-31 (ALSO READ VV. 23-29)

Several years ago, I was making a determined effort to become a better intercessor. I tried to give it more time, cover more needs, and pray with greater intensity. For a while things went well. Soon, however, I found myself skipping these extended prayer times when it wasn't convenient. But it bothered me that I could skip prayer so easily.

When I asked the Lord for insight on this, he helped me see that my problem was that I didn't really believe intercession changed anything. It seemed that life went on normally around me whether I prayed or not.

Then God brought me to Ezekiel 22. He showed me that intercessors, who by means of their prayers "build up the wall and stand . . . in the gap," are absolutely crucial to his government of the world. When I asked the question "Would the history of Israel have been different if God had found an intercessor?" I had to answer "yes." When I asked a further question, "Does the history of my family, church, or neighborhood depend on my intercession?" the answer again was "yes."

God seeks intercessors not because he lacks the wisdom or power to govern the world without them but because he, in his sovereign good pleasure, has chosen to govern the world through the prayers of his people. Intercession is not optional. It is a necessary and important part of God's way of working.

Things will happen when we pray that wouldn't have happened if we hadn't prayed. And things will not happen if we do not pray that would have happened if we had prayed.

In the New Testament era, God the Father always finds an intercessor to "build up the wall and stand before [him] in the gap." The One he finds is Jesus Christ, who ever lives to make intercession (Hebrews 7:25). But Christ does not pray alone. Our intercessory prayers are coupled with his. And he, by means of his Spirit, prays through us.

No wonder the kingdom is advancing and the gospel is spreading to every nation in the world. It's because of prayer. Are your prayers contributing to this worldwide thrust?

Reflect/Act

Try to imagine God determining what will happen in your family, on your block, in your church, or in your nation on the basis of your prayers. How does that make you feel?

What does this suggest about the importance of your role as an intercessor?

Prayer Starters for Praying Ezekiel 22:30-31

- *Praise* God for the greatness of his power and the wisdom of his choice to govern the world through the prayers of his people.
- *Confess* any failure at intercession that you are now aware of.
- *Thank* God for the awesome privilege of ruling the world with God through your prayers of intercession.
- *Ask* for grace to be a faithful intercessor.

Pray a BLESSing on those who live or work near you:

- **Body.** Ask the heavenly Father, who feeds the birds of the air (Matthew 6:26), to supply the food needs of your neighbors.
- **Labor.** Pray that employed neighbors will obey those who have authority over them with respect and sincerity of heart (Ephesians 6:5).
- **Emotional.** Pray that they may keep their lives "free from the love of money and be content" with what they have (Hebrews 13:5).
- **Social.** Pray for parents, asking that they will have the wisdom and ability to train up their children "in the way [they] should go" (Proverbs 22:6).
- **Spiritual.** Pray that Satan will not be able to blind the minds of your neighbors and keep them from seeing "the light of the gospel of the glory of Christ" (2 Corinthians 4:4).

Pray for specific needs of which you are aware.

DAY 6

THE SCOPE OF INTERCESSION

I urge, then, first of all, that requests, prayers, intercession and thanksgiving be made for everyone—for kings and all those in authority, that we may live peaceful and quiet lives in all godliness and holiness. This is good, and pleases God our Savior, who wants all men to be saved and to come to a knowledge of the truth. —1 TIMOTHY 2:1-4

E. M. Bounds said, "Prayer can do anything God can do." That's true because the only power in prayer is the power of God. What's more, prayer can reach anywhere God can reach. And God is everywhere, so his power can reach to every corner of the earth through our prayers.

Two phrases in the above verses emphasize the broad scope of prayer: "for everyone" and "all men [people]." Because God wants all people "to be saved and to come to a knowledge of the truth," he urges us to pray for everyone.

Ole Hallesby in his classic book *Prayer* grasps the heart of Paul's injunction: "It is our Lord's will that we who have received access to these powers through prayer should go through this world transmitting heavenly power to every corner of the world which needs it sorely. Our lives should be . . . quiet but steadily flowing streams of blessing, which through our prayers and intercessions should reach our whole environment" (p. 64).

When I sit in my favorite chair for my morning devotions, I imagine my prayers ascending to the throne room of heaven, and I imagine God, in response, moving his hands in the places where my prayers are directed. I imagine his power being released on the West Coast as I pray for family members, in our nation's capital as I pray for government officials, in foreign lands as I pray for mission enterprises, and in the homes and hearts of my neighbors as I pray for them. My prayers can release a blessing or bring change anywhere in the world without my moving from that chair. What an awesome power God has given us!

Though God would have us pray broad intercessory prayers, our prayer responsibilities start close to home. Our first responsibility is for immediate family members, then relatives and friends, then the spiritual family in which God has placed us, and then beyond that to our neighbors, community, nation, and world.

If our prayers focus only on those who are nearby, we have not caught the scope of what God intends through prayer. If they focus mainly on those far away, we may be guilty of failing to provide for our immediate families and of denying the faith (1 Timothy 5:4, 8).

Reflect/Act

Imagine your prayers transmitting heavenly power and blessing to people in every corner of the world. Think of some of those people and places.

Imagine persons experiencing the joy of being saved and coming to a knowledge of the truth as a result of your prayers.

Prayer Starters for Praying 1 Timothy 2:1-4

- *Praise* God, who is everywhere present in the universe.
- *Confess* to God your failure if your prayers have been too narrow and limited in comparison to the charge of 1 Timothy 2:1-4.
- *Thank* God for the breadth and depth of his concern for the world.
- *Commit* yourself to make "requests, prayers, intercession and thanksgiving . . . for everyone," including "kings and all those in authority."
- *Pray* that "all the ends of the earth will remember and turn to the Lord, and all the families of the nations will bow down before him" (Psalm 22:27).

Pray some broad prayers, using the following Bible verses. (Remember, though, that the nations begin at your doorsteps.)

- Pray that through Jesus Christ "all nations on earth will be blessed," as God promised Abraham in Genesis 22:18.
- Pray that "all the ends of the earth will remember and turn to the Lord, and all the families of all nations will bow before him" (Psalm 22:27).
- Pray that Isaiah 9:2—"The people walking in darkness have seen a great light; on those living in the land of the shadow of death a light has dawned"—will become a reality in lands that are still in the darkness of false religions.
- Pray that "every tongue [will] confess that Jesus Christ is Lord, to the glory of God the Father" (Philippians 2:11).

DAY 7

INTERCEDING FOR THE UNSAVED

Brothers, my heart's desire and prayer to God for the Israelites is that they may be saved. —ROMANS 10:1

The Bible clearly requires us to pray for persons who are not saved. In 1 Timothy 2 we are reminded that God wants all persons to be saved, and we are urged "therefore" to pray for everyone. Jesus modeled prayer for the unsaved when he prayed, "My prayer is not for [my disciples] alone. I pray also for those who will believe in me through their message" (John 17:20). And the apostle Paul was praying for the unsaved when he prayed his heart's desire for the Israelites (Romans 10:1).

How shall we pray for those who are not saved?

First, we should pray that the unsaved will be drawn by the Father. Jesus said, "No one can come to me unless the Father who sent me draws him" (John 6:44).

Second, we should pray that those who hear the gospel will understand it. Jesus warns that the evil one will come and snatch away the gospel seed sown in a person's heart if it is not understood (Matthew 13:19). The spiritual understanding and enlightenment required must come from God, who is moved to respond to the prayers of his people.

Third, we should pray that unbelievers' eyes will be opened so that they can see the light. As we pray this prayer, we will once again be contending with the adversary, "the god of this age [who] has blinded the minds of unbelievers, so that they cannot see the light of the gospel of the glory of Christ" (2 Corinthians 4:4). Opening spiritual eyes is, of course, God's business. But releasing God's power to open blinded eyes is prayer business, to which God calls us.

God honors prayer for the unsaved. A Lighthouse (an evangelistic home prayer group) in Grand Rapids, Michigan, prayed for a young man who had run away from home and joined a gang. The young man returned home and made a commitment to Christ. Later his grandfather gave his life to Christ shortly before he died, also in response to prayer.

Another Lighthouse in western Michigan saw four families come to the

Lord after eight months of weekly meetings to pray for their neighbors.

This is prayer evangelism, evangelism in which God moves in the hearts and lives of people in response to the earnest prayers of believers. Who among those who will believe in Christ are you praying for?

Reflect/Act

Do you care enough about the unsaved to pray earnestly for their salvation?

Would you care more if it were your own children or family members who were unsaved? Remember that all unsaved persons are wayward sons and daughters of God's family. God does not want "anyone to perish, but everyone to come to repentance" (2 Peter 3:9).

Prayer Starters for Praying Romans 10:1

- *Praise* God, who "so loved the world that he gave his one and only Son, that whoever believes in him shall . . . have eternal life" (John 3:16).
- *Thank* God for those who prayed for you and helped to open the door of salvation for you.
- If you do not have a burden for the unsaved, *ask* God to put such a burden on your heart.
- *Commit* yourself to partner with Jesus Christ in praying for persons yet to be saved.

Pray for unsaved persons, using the following Bible verses:

- Ask the Father to draw these persons to himself (John 6:44).
- Ask God to give them an understanding of the gospel and to forbid the devil from snatching away what is sown in their hearts (Matthew 13:19).
- Ask God to open their spiritual eyes, since "the god of this age has blinded the minds of unbelievers" (2 Corinthians 4:4).
- Pray for opportunities to relate to your neighbors where you are able to "be wise in the way you act toward outsiders" and to "make the most of every opportunity," with "your conversation . . . always full of grace, seasoned with salt, so that you may know how to answer everyone" (Colossians 4:5-6).

DAY 8

PRAYER RELEASES GOD'S POWER

The prayer of a righteous man is powerful and effective.
Elijah was a man just like us. He prayed earnestly that it would not
rain, and it did not rain on the land for three and a half years. Again
he prayed, and the heavens gave rain, and the earth produced its crops.
—JAMES 5:16-18

"Prayer," said C. Samuel Storms, "in and of itself possesses no power." I was astounded by that statement, and I didn't understand it until I read what Storms said next: "Prayer is powerful because God is powerful, and prayer is the means through which that divine power is released and channeled into our lives" (*Reaching God's Ear*, p. 223). In other words, all the power in prayer is really God's power, activated by prayer.

When you pray for another person, there is nothing that flows from you to them—no vibes, no force, no energy. Instead, your prayers go heavenward, and the power of God moves from him to the ones you pray for.

When the Bible says "prayer . . . is powerful and effective," it means God acts powerfully and effectively through the prayers of his people. Prayer is the instrument by which God has chosen to have his power directed in the universe. Ole Hallesby provides something of a mental picture of how this works: "This power is so rich and so mobile that all we have to do when we pray is to point to the persons or things to which we desire to have this power applied, and He, the Lord of this power, will direct the necessary power to the desired place" (*Prayer*, p. 63). What a surprising arrangement—God partnering with human beings to accomplish his purposes!

R. A. Torrey, enthralled by the enormity of this power, states, "Prayer is the key that unlocks all the storehouses of God's infinite grace and power. All that God is, and . . . has, is at the disposal of prayer. Prayer can do anything that God can do, and as God can do anything, prayer is omnipotent" (*The Power of Prayer*, p. 17).

Prayer can do what political action cannot, what education cannot, what military might cannot, and what planning committees cannot. All these are impotent by comparison.

Prayer can move mountains. It can change human hearts, families, neighborhoods, cities, and nations. It's the ultimate source of power, because it is the power of Almighty God. This power is available to the humblest Christian. It was "a man just like us" who prayed "that it would not rain," and God stopped the rain in Israel for three and a half years. Where will the power of your prayers be felt today?

Reflect/Act

Where do you think God would like some of his power directed through your prayers today?

What do you think God would like to do in your neighborhood or workplace in response to prayer?

Prayer Starters for Praying James 5:16-18
- *Praise* God for the great power by which he moves in our world and governs the affairs of all people.
- *Thank* God for his willingness to hear our prayers and to direct his power to places and persons through them.
- *Confess* if you have failed to make use of this great privilege to advance God's cause in this world through prayer.
- *Ask* God to help you become a powerful and effective pray-er.

Pray a BLESSing on those who live or work near you:
- **Body.** Thank God for his generous provision. "Give thanks to the Lord, for he . . . gives food to every creature. His love endures forever" (Psalm 136:1, 25).
- **Labor.** Pray that your neighbors may learn to work, doing something useful with their hands so that they "may have something to share with those in need" (Ephesians 4:28).
- **Emotional.** Pray that God will give them the "perfect peace" that comes from a steadfast mind and a trusting heart (Isaiah 26:3).
- **Social.** Pray that they may be sensitive to the needs of other around them and will have a desire to help and care for them.
- **Spiritual.** Pray that the Holy Spirit, who is sent to convict the world of sin, righteousness, and judgment (John 16:8), will work powerfully and effectively in the hearts and lives of unsaved people you pray for.

Pray for specific needs of which you are aware.

DAY 9

THE STRENGTH TO STAND

*Pray in the Spirit on all occasions with all kinds of prayers and
requests. With this in mind, be alert and always keep on praying
for all the saints.* —EPHESIANS 6:18

God has given us prayer so that we may help each other stand. The devil is always scheming to cause us to fall. But God provides ways to help us stand victorious over the powers of evil.

Paul warns us in Ephesians 6 against the devil's schemes and the "powers of this dark world" that are constantly opposing us. Four times he uses the word "stand" to encourage us to hold out against the onslaughts of the "spiritual forces of evil" (Ephesians 6:11-14).

Standing our ground requires that we first "put on the full armor of God." We are protected against the devil by knowing the truth, being righteous, having the gospel of peace, trusting God, possessing salvation, and using the Word of God in the right way. But Paul's order to "put on the full armor" does not end with "take . . . the sword of the Spirit, which is the word of God." It goes on without a break to say, "Pray in the Spirit on all occasions." In other words, the prayer support we give each other is an important part of our defense against the devil.

The prayer support required is all embracing. It's "on all occasions," of "all kinds," "always," and "for all the saints." Imagine being in the midst of a fellowship of Christians who prayed for each other this way. The possibility of falling would surely be minimized.

Several years ago, God led four other men and me to start a support group and to meet together every week for an hour and a half. We covenanted to share our lives with each other as fully as possible, study the Word of God faithfully, pursue God-given spiritual goals, and support each other in our daily prayers. What happened in the following months surprised us all. The first surprise was that almost every week one of us needed special prayer support to face a troublesome situation. Second, we all experienced spiritual growth of a kind that had eluded us in years past. And, third, every member of the group was launched into a key ministry position in the church or denomination within the next two years. As we stood together and supported each other in our daily prayers, God gave us the strength to stand and win victories.

God intends that all believers be strengthened to stand, as all take seriously the responsibility to always keep on praying, on all occasions, with all kinds of prayer for each other.

That's a tall order. It goes far beyond the kind of casual praying that most Christians are accustomed to. But those who pray "in the Spirit" can do it.

Reflect/Act

Do you sense that you are getting the kind of prayer support you need in order to stand?

Are you giving the believers around you the kind of prayer support they need in order to stand?

Is there anything more you should be doing to support the people around you in prayer? Be as specific as possible.

Prayer Starters for Praying Ephesians 6:18

- *Thank* God for his good and wise plan to supply prayer support for every member of his body. Thank him for people who have given you prayer support in the past—parents, grandparents, pastors, teachers, elders in the church, and many others.
- If you failed to provide prayer support for those who needed your prayers, *confess* that failure to God.
- *Ask* God to help the community of believers you are a part of to live up to the standard of Ephesians 6:18.
- *Commit* yourself to serious prayer support for the people around you.

Pray a BLESSing on those you live or work near:

- **Body.** Pray that God will provide for your neighbors, just as he "makes grass grow for the cattle, and plants . . . to cultivate—bringing forth food from the earth" (Psalm 104:14).
- **Labor.** Pray that their work may give them a sense of satisfaction. "The sleep of a laborer is sweet, whether he eats little or much" (Ecclesiastes 5:12).
- **Emotional.** Pray that they may be content because they have "learned

the secret of being content in any and every situation, whether well fed or hungry, whether living in plenty or in want" (Philippians 4:12).

- **Social.** Pray that they may "be kind and compassionate to one another, forgiving each other" (Ephesians 4:32).
- **Spiritual.** Pray that they will "put aside the deeds of darkness and put on the armor of light" (Romans 13:12).

Pray for specific needs of which you are aware.

DAY 10

PRAYER DEFEATS SATAN

"Simon, Simon, Satan has asked to sift you as wheat. But I have prayed for you, Simon, that your faith may not fail. And when you have turned back, strengthen your brothers." —LUKE 22:31-32

There are two powerful forces at work in the world today—the power of God and the power of Satan. The power of God is infinitely greater, but we are affected by both.

Satan, bent on our destruction, goes about "like a roaring lion looking for someone to devour" (1 Peter 5:8). God, intent on our salvation, supplies "everything we need for life and godliness" (2 Peter 1:3).

Since Satan's power is greater than ours, we are constantly at risk. Paul reminds us that we struggle "against the rulers, against the authorities, against the powers of this dark world and against the spiritual forces of evil" (Ephesians 6:12). But since God's power is greater than Satan's, we are safe in God's hands. God is our constant source of protection.

Prayer is the God-given means by which God's power is brought to our defense so that we can stand up against the devil's schemes. When Peter was being severely tested by Satan, Jesus came to his defense with prayer. He said, "I have prayed for you, Simon, that your faith may not fail."

We are engaged in a war that we must fight on our knees. Prayer is the power by which we are equipped to overcome the devil. To face him in our own strength is folly and a sure pathway to defeat.

The devil dreads our prayers more than anything else. A mighty prayer warrior once said, "Do you realize that there is nothing the devil dreads so much as prayer? His great concern is to keep us from praying. He loves to see us 'up to our eyes' in work—provided we do not pray. He does not fear if we are eager Bible students—provided we are little in prayer. Someone has wisely said, 'Satan laughs at our toiling, mocks at our wisdom, but trembles when we pray'" (*The Kneeling Christian*, p. 17).

It's no wonder that Satan trembles. By means of prayer the power of the omnipotent God of heaven and earth is brought against him. He doesn't stand a chance.

By prayer the kingdom of God is built, and by prayer the kingdom of Satan is destroyed. Where there is no prayer, there are no great works and there is no building of the kingdom. Pray much so that God may be glorified and his kingdom may come in all its fullness.

Reflect/Act

To what extent are you conscious that your prayers bring defeat to Satan's efforts?

Who among your acquaintances is now being tested by Satan and is in need of your prayers?

Prayer Starters for Praying Luke 22:31-32
- *Praise* the omnipotent God, who is able to destroy the works of the devil and protect his children.
- *Ask* Christ to teach you how to make use of prayer as a weapon to defeat Satan and to help advance God's kingdom.
- *Commit* yourself to prayerfully support the people around you, especially those whom you sense are under attack.

Pray for those who live or work near you, asking that God will set them free from the powers of evil.
- Ask God to set them free from bondage so that "they will come to their senses and escape from the trap of the devil, who has taken them captive to do his will" (2 Timothy 2:26).
- Pray that God will "open their eyes and turn them from darkness to light, and from the power of Satan to God, so that they may receive forgiveness of sins and a place among those who are sanctified by faith in [Jesus]" (Acts 26:18).
- Pray that the Son of God, who came "to destroy the devil's work" (1 John 3:8), may do so among your neighbors or fellow workers.

DAY 11

LOVING GOD FIRST

"Love the Lord your God with all your heart and with all your soul and with all your mind,' This is the first and greatest commandment. And the second is like it: 'Love your neighbor as yourself."
—Matthew 22:37-39

Have you ever wondered why you are on this planet? What plan does God have for you? Is there some larger purpose than making as good a living as possible, raising a family, making ends meet?

You bet there is! And Jesus summarizes that whole plan in one statement: Love God and love your neighbor. These are the two callings in your life. They are meant to be the foundation of all you do.

The next ten days of devotional reading in this book will help you focus on the second great commandment: loving your neighbor as yourself. But notice that this commandment flows from and is secondary to the first: loving God with all your heart.

Why is it important to love God with all your heart? Because if you are not close to the heart of God, you will not feel the strength and passion of God's love for your neighbors.

Let me illustrate with a story. Several years ago my son and I saw a small kitten on a farm, a "barn cat." It was bone-thin, with a swollen belly and infected eyes. Filled with pity for the little creature, and knowing it would not get medical treatment on the farm, we asked the farmer's permission to take it home.

The kitten was terrified. When we got home that evening, we made a large, secure box for it, filled with soft rags. We left it outside, covered, planning to take it to the vet in the morning.

That night I woke to the sound of thunder and pouring rain. I ran outside to bring the box under shelter—only to find the cover open and the box empty! I searched everywhere, not caring about the rain. All I could think of was a small, terrified kitten.

An hour later, I crawled back into bed, defeated. "Lord," I prayed over and over, "please help the kitten to be safe. Please don't let it wander away and starve. Save its life and help me to find it."

Then God spoke to my heart. "This is how I feel about your neighbors," he said. "I have the same passionate concern to save them from death. Do you have the same love for your neighbors as you do for that lost kitten?"

God taught me a powerful lesson that night. I could pray fervently for a lost kitten—but could I love my lost neighbors and pray fervently for them? I knew that if I were to love my neighbor, it would come through my drawing close enough to God's heart to feel his passion for them.

How close are you to God's heart? Do you love God enough to allow him to put his heart into yours? Are you willing to open yourself in prayer to receive God's heart for your neighbors? These next few days of devotions will challenge you to do that. But it will mean opening your heart to God first. —EB

Reflect/Act

How often do you think about the two great commandments during your day? What can you do to think about them more?

How can you grow in loving God "with all your heart and with all your soul and with all your mind"?

How can you grow in loving your neighbor as yourself?

Prayer Starters for Praying Matthew 22:37-39

- *Praise* God for his desire to have a love relationship with you.
- *Confess* any failure on your part to love God with all your heart and soul and mind, and ask him to remove things that get in the way of your loving him fully.
- *Thank* God for the compassionate love in his heart for you and for each person in your home and on your street.
- *Ask* God to draw you close enough to his heart to feel his passionate concern and overwhelming desire to save your neighbors from spiritual separation from him. Ask God to teach you how to love your neighbors as you love yourself and your family.

Pray a BLESSing on those who live or work near you:
- **Body.** Pray that God will make you aware of any physical limitations or illnesses your neighbors may have. Then ask God to use you to show his love in that circumstance or need.
- **Labor.** Pray that neighbors who work outside the home will meet Christians who show them the deep and passionate love of God.
- **Emotional.** Ask God to fill the empty spaces in unsaved neighbors' hearts with the knowledge that there is a God who loves them and wants them to love him in return.
- **Social.** Ask the Holy Spirit to make you sensitive to neighbors who may be looking for someone to talk to. Then ask the Spirit to teach you how to reach out in love to them.
- **Spiritual.** Pray that those who live on your street will be "rooted and established" in God's love and "have power . . . to grasp how wide and long and high and deep is the love of Christ" (Ephesians 3:17-18).

DAY 12

THE LOVE THAT NEVER FAILS

Love never fails. But where there are prophecies, they will cease; where there are tongues, they will be stilled; where there is knowledge, it will pass away. For we know in part and we prophesy in part, but when perfection comes, the imperfect disappears. —1 CORINTHIANS 13:8-10

There aren't many things in life about which you can say, "It never fails." A battery company claims to have a battery that never fails. Their untiring little bunny—the Energizer Bunny—goes on, and on, and on. But making a claim about something doesn't make it so. Media commercials and reality are two different things.

The apostle Paul's claim about love, though, is firmly rooted in reality. Love—the Bible's kind of love—doesn't fail. It doesn't fail because it is of God, whose nature is to love. God's love is different than human kinds of love. God's love flows to people who don't deserve it—unworthy people. It makes the ultimate sacrifice for them. "While we were still sinners, Christ died for us," says Paul in Romans 5:8.

When the apostle says, "Love never fails," he's not talking only about God's love; he's also talking about God's love in us and through us. Paul is reminding us that it's possible for us, with the love of God in our hearts, to love as God loves. Lewis Smedes defines this love as "the power that moves you to give to another person with no expectation of reward." Such love doesn't fail because it is not based on another person's behavior. Human love says, "I will keep loving you as long as you meet my needs, as long as you are well behaved, as long as you live up to my expectations." "Love that never fails" does not allow the behavior of another human being to interrupt its commitment to a life of love.

This is the way God expects us to relate to our neighbors, with never-failing love—a love that blesses, lifts, cares, and serves. There's power in that kind of love, a power that touches people's hearts and lives. It's a power that flows from God to us and through us to those whom we love. It's energized love. It cannot be stopped. It goes on, and on, and on.

A life of love is the only life truly worth living. A life without love amounts to "nothing but the creaking of a rusty gate" (*The Message,* 1 Corinthians 13:1).

You and I must first receive this kind of love from God. Then we are in a position to devote the rest of our lives to cultivating and freely giving this "love that never fails" to those around us. —AVG

Reflect/Act

Take time today to read 1 Corinthians 13 and consider what never-failing love means in your relationships with neighbors, work associates, and fellow students.

Think of one thing you can do to bless, lift, or serve a friend or neighbor.

Prayer Starters for Praying 1 Corinthians 13:8-10

- *Praise* God for his never-failing love to us.
- *Confess* the inadequacy of the conditional types of love we often show to the people around us.
- *Thank* God for people who, with never-failing love, have not given up on you.
- *Commit* yourself to living a life of never-failing love.

Pray a BLESSing on those who live or work near you:

- **Body.** Pray for neighbors who may be slaves to an addiction. Ask that God will restore them to freedom from whatever holds them in bondage and cripples their lives.
- **Labor.** Pray for neighbors who may feel useless because they are unable to work. Ask God to help them focus on what they still can do, and to show them that our worth is not found in what we do but in who we are.
- **Emotional.** Pray for lonely people whose life situations make them feel isolated. Ask God to help you draw them into vibrant friendship with Jesus Christ.
- **Social.** Pray for parents whose responsibilities sometimes seem overwhelming, that they may receive the help they need to be good parents.
- **Spiritual.** Pray that neighbors may, by the grace of God, come to treasure the Lord and love him with all their heart, soul, and mind.

DAY 13

BEING THE FRAGRANCE OF CHRIST

*Thanks be to God, who . . . through us spreads everywhere the fragrance
of the knowledge of him. For we are to God the aroma of Christ among
those who are being saved and those who are perishing. To the one we
are the smell of death; to the other, the fragrance of life. And who is
equal to such a task?* —2 CORINTHIANS 2:14-16

I went to my neighbor's house to return a book last week. When I entered her house, I was enveloped in the aroma of a casserole she had just taken from the oven. The fragrance was welcoming, warm, and inviting. My taste buds began to water, and I realized I was hungry. Before she even said a word, I was wishing for an invitation to dinner.

Aromas can subtly yet powerfully influence our feelings and thoughts. We cannot see or touch odors, but their presence is unmistakable. Perfume makers know the power of a warm, alluring scent. Real estate agents tell their sellers to sprinkle cinnamon in their ovens and turn the heat on low, to create a warm and homey scent of baking in the home as potential buyers come through.

Did you know there's a spiritual fragrance as well? The love of Christ in the hearts of Christians is a subtle, invisible, yet unmistakable aroma of the Spirit of God. Others may notice it even before you speak to them. They experience it in the acceptance and friendliness of your manner.

What's the source of this fragrance? It comes from spending time with God. It's the love that clings to you when you come from being in God's presence, through prayer and reflection on the Scriptures.

It's the aroma of the Spirit described in 1 Corinthians 13—a patient, kind, selfless nature that "always protects, always trusts, always hopes, always perseveres" (13:7). This loving Spirit within you comes from Jesus, from spending time with him, resting in his love for you, and hearing his words of assurance and instruction in the Bible. This is the aroma your neighbors and the people you work with will notice about you. It's what will attract them to you, encourage them to trust you, and make them want to spend time with you.

As our Scripture passage for this devotion points out, some people will not find the fragrance of God's love appealing; instead they will find it displeasing. That's okay—it doesn't mean you are doing something wrong; it just means they are fighting against God's work in their lives. Keep showing them God's love.

When you wear a fragrance, you have to get close enough to people to allow them to smell it. What can you do to get closer to your neighbors—close enough that they can sense the presence of Christ around and within you? Do you share hobbies? Is there a chore you can do for a neighbor who is experiencing illness or hardship? Do you make time to have families over for dessert and conversation? Can you offer to take some of their children with you to the lake or to a good movie? Find ways to spend time and get to know the people God has placed around you—and let them get to know you. You must, as Paul did, open your heart wide to them (2 Corinthians 6:11).

"And who is equal to such a task?" You are, if you take time each day to bathe in the fragrance of God's love. That fragrance will be more compelling and inviting on you than the most expensive perfume. —EB

Reflect/Act

What people have shown you the fragrant love of Christ in their lives?

What people around you need more of that fragrance in their lives? How can you show it to them?

Allow yourself space and time each day to seek and experience God's love for you in Christ. How will that experience affect the "aroma" you spread to others who are close to you during the day?

Prayer Starters for Praying 2 Corinthians 2:14-16

- *Praise* God for the overpowering greatness and sweetness of his love for you and for others.
- *Confess* to God any situations in the past week in which you gave off an aroma different from that of Christ's love. Ask the Spirit to show you how you may need to ask forgiveness of others as well as of God.
- *Thank* God for the wonderful opportunity to share in spreading the aroma of Jesus' love.
- *Ask* God for the time and energy to grow closer to your neighbors and

co-workers and for the wisdom to identify those who will find his love a fragrance that leads to life.

Pray a BLESSing on your neighbors, using Psalm 138:6-8:
- Pray that your neighbors will realize the need to be humble before God, that his love is toward the humble rather than the proud.
- Ask God to preserve your neighbors' spiritual and emotional health, even as they "walk in the midst of trouble."
- Pray that God's purpose for the life of your neighbors will be fulfilled, and that they may find the aroma of God's love for them in Christ Jesus.
- Pray that your neighbors' eyes may be opened to see the love of God that endures forever, and to find the security that God will never abandon them.

DAY 14

ENTERTAINING STRANGERS

Do not forget to entertain strangers, for by so doing some people have entertained angels without knowing it. —HEBREWS 13:2

They were standing in the corner out of everyone's way—a refugee family from Bosnia, though I didn't know it at the time. Someone had invited them to our church, and they had come, hoping to make some connections in this strange new land.

Though the foyer was milling with people, I saw no one stop and speak to this man, his wife, or their three daughters. I walked toward them and heard them speaking to each other in a language other than English. *What if they can't understand me?* I thought. I felt awkward and foolish. But I went to meet them anyway.

When I said hello, the man's face broke into a smile. He introduced his wife and daughters to me, in broken English. The wife could only say, "Hello," but she smiled as warmly as her husband. I found that the daughters, though shy, spoke English fairly well, and we talked briefly before the service. I invited them to sit with our family, and we helped them through the songs and liturgy.

After church, I introduced them to another family and then, mentally taking a quick inventory of my freezer contents, invited everyone to lunch for hot dogs and coleslaw. Not very fancy, but we sat out on the deck and talked about the war in Bosnia, how to find jobs, what schools were best, Dutch and Bosnian recipes, and where to find a better rental house (theirs had cockroaches).

We became firm friends. For two years now, our friends from a faraway land have been bringing over their wonderful meat pastries, fresh fish caught on weekend fishing trips, and, best of all, just their happiness to spend time with us. Their loyalty and dedication to our friendship far surpasses any that we have experienced among our North American friends.

We found that we had "entertained angels without knowing it." The point of our Scripture for this devotion is that God is watching how we treat his loved ones, especially those in need. (See also Matthew 25:34-40.)

Had I allowed our differences and my fear to keep me from approaching these people, we would have missed being a blessing to each other.

People from foreign lands are strangers. But you don't have to look for a refugee family to find a stranger. Who on your street is a stranger to you? Is there someone who has left home and family—whether in Ohio or Mexico or British Columbia—and moved into your neighborhood? Is there an individual or family who keep themselves aloof from neighborhood gatherings—a self-imposed stranger? Is there a lonely widower who has begun to find comfort in alcohol? A refugee family moving into a nearby apartment or taking a new position at work? A newly divorced parent with children?

To open your home to such an individual or family is a wonderful gift that shows God's warm and outreaching love to a stranger. It doesn't take much. Try to keep something in the freezer that you can cook up quickly for last-minute invitations. I have found that our guests are far more interested in a warm invitation and good conversation than the quality of the food served.

Your invitation may open the door of God's family to "the stranger" on your street or at your workplace. What a wonderful way to meet "angels"! —EB

Reflect/Act

What makes you hesitate to extend an invitation? Is it fear, awkwardness, overbusyness, lack of resources?

Identify that last time you invited a stranger into your home. Make plans to invite over someone you don't know very well in the next two weeks, out of hospitality for Jesus' sake.

Prayer Starters for Praying Hebrews 13:2

- *Praise* God for his openhearted hospitality and generosity to all living things (Psalm 145:15-16).
- *Confess* situations in which you may have placed your needs inappropriately ahead of the needs of a stranger looking for hospitality.
- *Thank* God for the strangers he has placed in your life—on your street or at work—as opportunities to show his loving hospitality.
- *Ask* God for the faith or vision to see that encounters with strangers can turn into blessings.

Pray a BLESSing on the people around you, using Psalm 145:8-21:

- Ask God to pour his grace, rich love, compassion, and goodness into these neighbors' lives, and to be slow to anger about their sins.
- Pray that these neighbors will come into contact with someone who will tell them of the glory of God's kingdom and speak of God's mighty acts. (Pray that God lets you be the one to share his grace with them.)
- Ask God to lift up neighbors who may have fallen or who may be "down."
- Ask the Holy Spirit to be near to these people when they call out to God, that he will hear their cry and save them.

DAY 15

BEING WISE TOWARD OUTSIDERS

Be wise in the way you act toward outsiders; make the most of every opportunity. Let your conversation be always full of grace, seasoned with salt, so that you may know how to answer everyone.
—COLOSSIANS 4:5-6

There are two people I've gotten to know better than almost anyone besides my immediate family and my prayer group. One is a woman at work, and one is a neighbor who lives two doors down. One is a Christian, and one is not.

The reason I've gotten to know them so well is that they are my walking partners. With one, I walk once a week on my lunch hour; with the other, I walk on weekends or summer evenings. We put on our old walking shoes, wear a jacket in cool weather, and spend about an hour stretching our legs—and talking with each other.

These weekly conversations have opened windows for us into each other's lives. I have been able to share my faith, as well as the daily enjoyments and frustrations of life. I have had ample opportunity to let my conversation be "full of grace, seasoned with salt," to my neighbor who is outside the church, as well as to my sister in Christ at work.

Conversations with both of these friends are a pleasure and an encouragement. With my neighbor I talk about gardening, crime prevention efforts in our neighborhood, our struggles with parenting teenage children, neighbors whose son is dying of AIDS, and sometimes even the frequent hypocrisy and close-mindedness of "religious" people.

I also pray especially before walking with her—perhaps because I know that ultimately so much is at stake. I pray that God will accompany us with his Spirit and will give me wisdom as I talk.

I have prayed that my neighbor will ask questions that provide an opening for me to share what I've learned about God through the Bible and through my own life as a Christian. I pray that I will not be afraid to have "salty" conversation—in other words, to say things that are distinctly different from the way the rest of the world looks at life.

Sometimes I feel a bit inadequate in this. What if my neighbor's knowledge of the Christian faith is based entirely on her acquaintance with me? I remember the Apostle Paul's words: "Who is equal to such a task?" (2 Corinthians 2:16). But I also remember Paul's encouragement from the same passage: "But thanks be to God, who always leads us in triumphal procession in Christ and through us spreads everywhere the fragrance of the knowledge of him" (2:14). It's comforting to know that God has chosen weak and flawed believers like me to be salt and light to unbelievers, and that he provides what is needed for such work.

The verses from Colossians 4 above assume, of course, that there will be opportunities for conversation between you and "outsiders." Have you made time in your life for such opportunities? Are you willing to do so? You may be the only salt and light that they come into contact with. –EB

Reflect/Act

Why is it important to be careful in your conversation with outsiders?

In what areas of your life do you have close personal contact with an outsider? Think of at least two ways in which you can increase that contact in the coming week.

Prayer Starters for Praying Colossians 4:5-6

- *Praise* God for his ability to impart wisdom through the Holy Spirit.
- *Confess* that in conversations with unbelievers you may have been unwise in what you said or you may have missed an opportunity to share the good news of Jesus.
- *Thank* God for calling you to act as a seasoning and as a preservative in this world.
- *Ask* God to fill you with his grace and give you opportunities to speak to outsiders.

Pray a BLESSing for your neighbors, using Romans 10:14-17

- Pray that God will send people into your neighbors' lives to speak the good news to them, if they don't have a relationship with Jesus.
- Pray that when your neighbors hear the good news about Jesus, they will believe and commit their lives to him.
- Pray that this faith will change their lives so that they, in turn, may bring the good news to others.

DAY 16

THE NEED TO BE NEEDED

When a Samaritan woman came to draw water, Jesus said to her, "Will you give me a drink?" —JOHN 4:7

It was a huge cabin cruiser, not something you'd ever think of building in a backyard. But my friend did it. It took him three years to build. Having virtually no mechanical ability myself, I was overwhelmed.

"How did you do it?" I asked. "Did you really figure out everything yourself? Didn't you have any plans?"

"No," my pastor friend replied, "I didn't have any plans, and I figured it all out by myself. Except, that is, for one thing. I could not figure out how to drill that long hole through the beam for the propeller shaft. That was too much."

Then he told me a fascinating story connected with that problem. God used it to bring a very difficult character into his family.

"I had witnessed to one of my neighbors many times, but whatever I would say about Christianity fell on totally deaf ears. This fellow was just not interested. And there was no way I could reach out to him. He was proudly independent. He had been a carpenter all his life—a very skilled carpenter.

"When I tried to figure out how to get that hole drilled, the Lord put his name into my mind. I realized at that moment that maybe my neighbor's greatest need was to be needed! I could ask him if he knew how to drill that long hole for my propeller shaft.

"Wow, what a breakthrough! All the hard shell in my neighbor's character dropped away when I put myself in a position of needing his services. I offered to pay for his time, of course, but my request to him drew him into my project. Over the next few months we were drawn into a deep friendship. It was that friendship that opened the door of his heart. Since I had dignified him and in that way met his need of being needed, he was profoundly grateful and listened as I shared the message of the Savior with him. He became a faithful and active member of the church."

This was the same approach Jesus used when he met the Samaritan woman at the well. He recognized that her greatest need was the need to be needed, the need for dignity. He met that need when he asked her for a drink of water. And she was surprised! She could barely believe that a man, a Jewish man, would ask a favor of a woman, especially a Samaritan woman. Jesus dignified her by asking her to help him.

When we think of caring, we almost immediately think of people who need something. Then we give them something even though they might really need the opposite. To really care for people means that we sensitively look for something they have to offer; it means we try to fill their "need to be needed" by asking for a favor that we know a person can do and that this person enjoys doing.

When you ask God to show you how to care, be certain not just to look at what you might give to your neighbor. Also ask God to show you how to dignify your neighbor by allowing him or her to give to you. —JDV

Reflect/Act

Think of some specific ways in which others could help you.

Intentionally ask for help today. It could be something very small. Be alert to how you feel in asking and how the other person responds.

Prayer-Starters for Praying John 4:7
- *Thank* God that he dignified you with important things for you to do for him.
- *Confess* if you have not recognized the need of others to be needed.
- *Ask* God to help you dignify others with appropriate requests for help.

Pray a BLESSing on those who live or work near you:
- **Body.** Pray that your neighbors and co-corkers may keep their bodies fit as temples of the Holy Spirit (1 Corinthians 6:19).
- **Labor.** Pray that God will give these neighbors many opportunities to make use of the skills and talents he has given them.
- **Emotional.** Pray for those who feel useless because they have not found their niche in life or have not found a way to use their skills and talents meaningfully.
- **Social.** Ask the Lord to provide meaningful friends and relationships for those who are lonely.
- **Spiritual.** Pray that your neighbors and fellow employees may come to know their true worth in God's eyes and may be drawn to him.

DAY 17

LOVING YOUR ENEMY

"You have heard that it was said, 'Love your neighbor and hate your enemy.' But I tell you: Love your enemies and pray for those who persecute you, that you may be sons of your Father in heaven. He causes his sun to rise on the evil and the good, and sends rain on the righteous and the unrighteous. If you love those who love you, what reward will you get?" —MATTHEW 5:43-46

I have to admit that my co-worker and I have a hard time getting along. She and I have very different personalities, and we find it difficult to understand each other. On some issues at the office, we find ourselves as opponents, not colleagues. Some unkind words have been said, and, as a result, there is friction. Though we are outwardly polite, underneath is often a feeling of tension.

The situation has not been easy for me to deal with. Daily contact with a person who has sometimes treated me unfairly (in my estimation) and has spoken ill of me to others is not pleasant. From time to time we have attempted to talk things out, but so far that has only worsened the situation.

For a while resentment built up in my heart. Though outwardly polite, I inwardly nurtured a dislike of my co-worker and daily reviewed a list of grievances. Though I prayed for my co-worker and myself, I was at a loss for what to do. Should I be aggressive and accusing? Should I stuff down my feelings and pretend everything was okay?

Then I read this: "The Lord's servant must not quarrel; instead, he must be kind to everyone, able to teach, not resentful. Those who oppose him he must gently instruct, in the hope that God will grant them repentance leading them to a knowledge of the truth" (2 Timothy 2:24-25).

Those words leaped off the page. I instantly prayed: "Lord, take away my resentful heart. Teach me how to instruct gently, without anger or condescension. Use me in any way you wish to lead my co-worker to a knowledge of the truth that you are real and that you love her."

God answered my prayer quickly. He somehow took the sting of resentment from within my heart (what a miracle the working of the Spirit is!). Nothing has changed in the way my co-worker treats me, but I have a spirit of love and gentleness that was not there before. I no longer feel threatened by my co-worker. Instead, I have a sense of expectation that God will continue to work in both her and me.

I am waiting for the Spirit's opportunity and prompting, and I will continue to pray for peace in our relationship. I am looking for ways to care for her.

God has a plan for his people: to show that he loves all people, even the unjust and the unkind. In order to be mirror images of Jesus, we are to love our enemies and pray for those who persecute us. For a graphic example of this kind of love, simply look at Jesus on the cross.

Who in your life has become an irritant, an opponent, someone who seems to be out to get you? Have you asked God to send his sunshine into that person's life? Have you asked God to pour his love into your heart? When you do this, miracles begin to happen. —EB

Reflect/Act

Is it fair of God to ask that you love your enemy? Why or why not?

Let God bring to mind someone who has hurt you, someone whom you now regard as an enemy. How might it be possible to love someone who has slandered and worked against you? What would you need in order to be able to do this? Ask God to show you one thing you can do this week to show love to your enemy.

Prayer Starters for Praying Matthew 5:43-46

- *Praise* God for his loving-kindness, which is poured out on believers and unbelievers alike.
- *Ask* God to show you any times when your love and kindness may have been limited to those who have been loving toward you. Confess those shortcomings, and seek God's forgiveness, remembering also to forgive others who have wronged you (Matthew 6:14-15).
- *Thank* Jesus for the example he gave of loving his enemies and commit yourself to following his example.

Pray a BLESSing on your neighbors and co-workers:

- **Body.** Pray that God will provide your neighbors and co-workers with the basic needs for living (Matthew 6:21-31).

- **Labor.** Ask God to bless their efforts at work and to prosper the use of their gifts and talents.
- **Emotional.** Ask God to fill any emotional needs through the Holy Spirit so that these neighbors may be filled with the Lord's loving-kindness.
- **Social.** Ask God to use your relationships with your neighbors and co-workers to reflect his amazing, abundant, and forgiving love.
- **Spiritual.** Pray that these persons may grow by God's Spirit to show true humility, selflessness, and love (Philippians 2:2-4).

DAY 18

PRAYER, CARE, ACTION

Jesus looked up and said, "Father, I thank you that you have heard me. I knew that you always hear me, but I said this for the benefit of the people standing here, that they may believe that you sent me." When he had said this, Jesus called in a loud voice, "Lazarus, come out!" —JOHN 11:41-43

In the middle of each Lighthouse seminar I lead, I ask participants to write down the names of five neighbors, work associates, or acquaintances and to spend five minutes, right there, praying for them. After the prayer time I ask, "What did you experience in your prayer time?"

The responses people give, as they tell the whole group about these brief experiences, always amaze me. They tell of feeling "compassion," "love welling up," "burden," "empathy," and "gratitude" for the neighbors they have prayed for. They said they "are drawn to them," "want to get to know them," and "are motivated to do something." They see themselves as "divinely positioned to reach out" to their neighbors and "ready to take time with them." They become aware of their neighbors' "lostness" and "that they matter to God." All of this takes place in just five minutes of prayer.

What becomes clear to me through responses to this exercise is that praying leads to caring—or, to say it the other way around, caring flows out of praying. As water in an artesian well flows naturally to the surface, so love flows naturally from the heart of a "pray-er"—and motivation to action soon follows.

Jesus' raising of Lazarus begins with prayer. He has been praying about Lazarus even before he arrives in Bethany, for he says, "Father, I thank you that you have heard me." And as he arrives, Jesus' loving, caring concern for his friends is evident. He is "deeply moved in spirit" (v. 33), and moments later he is in tears (v. 35). Soon, though, he is taking action as he stands by Lazarus's grave and calls for him to "come out."

In Jesus we see a prayer-care-action pattern that is meant to be followed as we reach out to our neighbors and friends. We begin by praying.

Then caring follows as love for them wells up in our hearts. And then we are motivated to act in some way on our neighbors' behalf.

Caring begins in prayer. As you pray for your neighbors, be alert to what happens in your own heart. Do you feel compassion? Do you feel a burden for their spiritual well-being? Do you feel drawn to them? Are you ready to spend some time with them? Do you sense how much they matter to God?

Then action flows from caring. Are you motivated to do something for them? Follow the promptings of your heart as the Spirit of God leads you to reach out in caring ways to the people around you. Act on their behalf in ways that show the love of Christ. This is the biblical pattern. —AVG

Reflect/Act

Identify and write down the feelings that surface as you pray for your friends and neighbors.

Act on the promptings you believe to be in line with God's will.

Prayer Starters for Praying John 11:41-43

- *Thank* God for his willingness to hear our prayers for others and to use us in providing for their needs.
- *Confess* any uncaring attitudes toward neighbors that you may have had.
- *Ask* God to fill your heart with love for those around you and to motivate you to act with love on their behalf.
- *Commit* yourself to act on behalf of others as the Holy Spirit prompts you.

Pray a BLESSing on your neighbors or co-workers:

- **Body.** Pray for these neighbors' physical health and strength.
- **Labor.** Pray that their work at home, at school, or on the job may be stimulating and satisfying.
- **Emotional.** Pray that the peace of God that surpasses understanding will guard your neighbors' hearts and minds in Christ Jesus (Philippians 4:7).
- **Social.** Pray for many positive, loving, supportive relationships in your neighbors' lives.
- **Spiritual.** Pray that your neighbors may come to know Jesus Christ as Lord and Savior or that their faith in Christ may be strengthened.

DAY 19

LISTENING TO GOD

"When he, the Spirit of truth, comes, he will guide you into all truth.
He will not speak on his own; he will speak only what he hears, and he
*will tell you what is yet to come." —*JOHN 16:13

How can you tell when God speaks to you? Do you ever wonder about people who confidently say, "Well, God told me to" do this or that? How do they know?

Without a doubt there is spiritual abuse among people who claim to hear God talking to them. But the Bible tells us clearly that Jesus' gift to us as believers is the Spirit of God within us. And since the Spirit lives both in the mind of the Father and in our own minds, he can communicate and guide us with the very thoughts of God. The only problem is to find how we can know that the ideas we get are not from our own sinful nature or from the devil but from God. Here's a true story that shows a way in which some missionaries have heard God speaking to their hearts.

Mary Ghee was a missionary to India in the 1950s. She worked as a teacher for almost two years in a village, but had little success bringing anyone to Christ. Then Dr. Scudder, a missionary doctor, visited the village for a week. During his visit many amazing things happened. This perplexed Mary's Indian neighbors. "Why," they asked her, "does your God work miracles when Dr. Scudder comes? You have been among us for nearly two years, and yet very few things have happened." How would you respond?

Mary asked Dr. Scudder what he did. The doctor said that whenever he presented a problem to the Lord, he would ask God to "shut off" his sinful desires and the voice of the devil. Then he would wait, and he would write down the first thing that came to his mind. And if it was in line with Scripture, he concluded that God was speaking to him. So he went out and did it.

Mary was having a problem with her neighbor, so early one morning she tried this approach as she prayed. "God," she prayed, "I am going to listen and write down the first thing you tell me to do to solve this problem with my neighbor." She waited, with pencil and paper ready. Suddenly a thought came: *Take her an egg.* Mary thought about this. Her neighbor was a widow with ten children. How embarrassing it would be to take just one egg! So she wrinkled up the paper, threw it away, and went to do her teaching for the morning.

That noon, when she came home, Mary found that a chicken had found its way into her house and was resting on one of her chairs. Then, when she shooed it away, she saw that it had laid an egg on the chair. "All right, Lord," Mary said. "I get the message." She took the egg to her neighbor's house and gave it to one of the woman's little boys, who was playing outside.

The next morning the neighbor came to Mary's house and asked, "Why did you give me that egg yesterday, Mary?" With embarrassment, Mary told her how she had been trying to listen to the Lord to solve the problem they were having. "Mary!" said her neighbor excitedly. "You know how poor I am. Yesterday I had given all my food to my children. In the morning I prayed, 'God, if you would only give me one egg, I can make it through the day.' God used you to bring me that egg!" From that point on, Mary and her neighbor stopped their fighting. God worked his miracle of reconciliation.

Don't discount an answer you may be receiving from God because it seems not to make any sense. God answers us in many ways, and we can always search his Word, the Bible, for guidance when we think we hear God speaking to us. Just be aware that God may be speaking to you in surprising ways. Remember Joshua and the battle of Jericho (Joshua 5:13-27). Remember Gideon (Judges 6-7). Remember Peter and Cornelius (Acts 10).

As long as the answer you hear seems to help or show love to someone, do what God gently inclines your mind to do in caring for others. Some very imaginative things may happen. But don't be afraid to follow your inclinations, for God may have some marvelous surprises in store for you. —JDV

Reflect/Act

Reflect briefly on the fact that God knows the answers to all your questions. Ask God for guidance on a specific concern you have and then give him time to impress you with his thoughts as you wait.

Prayer Starters for Praying John 16:13

- *Praise* God, who guides us into all truth.
- *Confess* to the Lord any tendency you may have to move ahead on your own without seeking his guidance.
- *Commit* all your ways to the Lord
- *Ask* to be filled with the knowledge of God's will.

Pray a BLESSing on your neighbors, using Proverbs 3:5-7:

- Pray that your neighbors will learn to "trust in the Lord with all [their] heart and lean not on [their] own understanding."
- Pray that your neighbors will acknowledge the Lord in all their ways.

DAY 20

REACHING OUT A HAND

This is how we know what love is: Jesus Christ laid down his life for us. And we ought to lay down our lives for our brothers. If anyone has material possessions and sees his brother in need but has no pity on him, how can the love of God be in him? —1 JOHN 3:16-17

"The beautiful IDS Building towers over the skyline of Minneapolis. Its fifty-seven stories of blue-black glass make an impressive sight.

One day, a depressed executive opened the doors of his fifteenth-story office, walked out on the ledge, and threatened to leap to his death.

A Christian friend, who happened to be present, pleaded with the man not to take his own life.

Teetering on the edge, the executive said, 'If you really mean it—will you come over and take my hand?'

The Christian man, realizing his friend could drag both of them over the edge—hesitated.

When the businessman saw the hesitation, he said, 'You're just like the rest. You talk, but you don't really care.' Then he turned and leaped to his death."

—adapted from *Heart for the Harvest* by Lowell Lundstrom

What Jesus did for us was more than talk. It was more than showing us how to live as God wants us to. He really cared! He cared so much for us that he "laid down his life for us." Finding us in a hopeless state of despair and spiritual death, Jesus reached out his hand and drew us back to safety. "This is how we know what love is."

Jesus now asks us to be willing to do for others as he did for us. "We ought to lay down our lives for our brothers," says John. That's a mighty big challenge!

Does this mean we have to die to prove our love for others? No, although some of us may be called to die to show our love for Jesus. John is talking here about being willing, for Jesus' sake, to do whatever is necessary to meet the needs of those around us, even to the point of death. He is challenging us to *really* care! When we're that willing and that ready to care, we will truly reflect the love of Christ.

Caring that goes beyond talk, to reaching out a hand, is risky business. We risk being pulled off the "comfort ledge" of our lives into something that may be costly. It may cost us time. It may cost us energy. It may require giving up some of our treasured freedom. It may also cost us money or material goods.

Our willingness to part with something we value for Jesus' sake and to give it to people who are in need is a sign that the love of God is in us. This is how love shows itself. The evidence is on display in whatever we do.

We live in a very hurting world. It's a world full of opportunities to care, and in our caring, we have all kinds of opportunities to showcase Jesus' love to the people around us.

Is there a showcase of God's love in your neighborhood? —AVG

Reflect/Act

Think of a time when someone reached out a hand to you. What does it tell you about that person? About God?

Think of needs and hurts in the lives of the people around you that may give you an opportunity to reach out to them.

Prayer Starters for 1 John 3:16-17
- *Praise* Jesus for the love that caused him to lay down his life for you. Thank him for doing that.
- *Confess* any failing you may have had in reaching out a loving hand to another person.
- *Ask* God to help you see the needs of people around you and to give you a heart willing to pay the cost of reaching out.

Pray a BLESSing on those who live or work near you:
- **Body.** Offer yourself to be used by God to help meet the needs of the people around you.
- **Labor.** Pray that neighbors will work diligently and handle their financial resources wisely so that they may give of their resources to reach out to others.
- **Emotional.** Pray that hurting people may have the grace to admit

their need for help and allow others to help them.

- **Social.** Pray that parents may be willing to give of themselves for their children, and that friends and neighbors may be willing to give of themselves for each other.
- **Spiritual.** Pray that your neighbors will come to know God's love and be willing to take hold of his loving hand outstretched to them.

DAY 21

I'M TERRIFIED

*Moses said to the Lord, "O Lord, I have never been eloquent,
neither in the past nor since you have spoken to your servant.
I am slow of speech and tongue."
The Lord said to him, "Who gave man his mouth? Who makes him
deaf or mute? Who gives him sight or makes him blind? Is it not I, the
Lord? Now go; I will help you speak and will teach you what to say."*
—EXODUS 4:10-12

'll admit it, first thing: Sharing with my neighbors terrifies me. That's right. I pray for my neighbors; I care about them. But to share my faith with them just downright terrifies me.

I'm not sure I even understand why. In the past, I've talked with my neighbors about politics. They know what I do professionally. We've shared lawn and carpentry tools. I've brought them meals when they've been sick; they've returned the favor. I've visited them when they've been hospitalized. Some of us even exchange Christmas and birthday cards and gifts. We know a lot about each other's families and friends. I've even been asked to officiate at memorial services for family pets. But, for some reason, talking with my neighbors about my relationship with Christ is something that makes my heart go into overdrive.

There are a lot of reasons for this, I suppose. God is very important to me, and I want my neighbors to know about him—but what if I give them the wrong information? And what approach do I take? I certainly don't want to come off as "preachy." And what if I completely blow it? I may only get one chance. If I don't get it right, there goes their whole eternity!

There are lots of reasons why we don't share our faith with our neighbors. But one of the main reasons is that we are just too afraid. And our fear may come from a notion that sharing our faith puts us in a position of too much responsibility—more than we can handle. We don't feel capable of helping God bring the miracle of new life. Some of us really believe that it's up to us alone to bring our neighbors into a personal relationship with God.

As you begin to move from praying, to caring, to actually sharing the good news of Jesus with your neighbor, always remember who takes the ultimate responsibility for your neighbor's response. It's not you. The one responsible for the miracle of new life is God alone.

Through his Holy Spirit, God is already at work in the heart of your neighbor. And God is already at work in you. Your job is simply to be available as the voice box for the words the Holy Spirit will give you to speak. You aren't the one who will change your neighbor's heart. You aren't the one who will cause him or her to cross the line from disbelief to belief in Jesus. That's God's job. He simply invites you to work along-side him.

Reflect/Act

How responsive are you to the leading of God the Holy Spirit in your life?

What are some of the specific ways in which God has done an unexpected, miraculous thing in your life?

Prayer Starters for Praying Exodus 4:10-12
- *Praise* God by letting him know how thankful you are that he is in control. God is the one who gave you your mouth, your mind, your eyes, your ears. God is the one who has a perfect plan for your life and for the lives of your neighbors.
- *Ask* God to calm your fears and settle your anxieties about sharing with your neighbor. Ask him to give you the words to speak.
- *Thank* God that he loves you and your neighbor more than any of us could ever imagine. The Lord's desire is to share eternity with us. He has done everything necessary to make that possible.

Pray a BLESSing on those who live or work near you:
Remember that the word *BLESS* here serves as a reminder of five vital areas in our lives.
- **Body.** Pray that you may be a blessing to your neighbors by helping with any physical needs they might have.
- **Labor.** Ask God to help your neighbors serve him through their work today, doing all they can to the glory of God (Colossians 3:23).
- **Emotional.** Ask that your neighbors may not be burdened by any

worries or anxieties but have "the peace of God, which transcends all understanding" (Philippians 4:7).

- **Social.** Ask God to provide opportunities for your neighbors to meet with and talk with believers like you about Jesus and his good news.
- **Spiritual.** Pray that your unsaved neighbors will come to know Christ through faithful witnesses of his love. Ask that God will use you to share the good news of Jesus with your neighbors.

DAY 22

ON BEYOND ZEBRA

Jesus said . . . "How hard it is to enter the kingdom of God!
It is easier for a camel to go through the eye of a needle than for a
rich man to enter the kingdom of God."
The disciples . . . said to each other, "Who then can be saved?"
Jesus . . . said, "With man this is impossible, but not with God;
*all things are possible with God." —*MARK 10:24-27

'm a little embarrassed to say this, but one of my favorite authors is Theodor Geisel, also known as Dr. Seuss. That's right—one of my favorite authors is a children's writer. Dr. Seuss was a master of helping us to see and understand big and amazing things in simple, childlike ways.

One of my favorite stories by Dr. Seuss is *On Beyond Zebra!*. In this story a boy is showing another boy how to spell: "The A is for Ape. And the B is for Bear. The C is for Camel. The H is for Hare. The M is for Mouse. And the R is for Rat. I know all the twenty-six letters like that." But that wasn't enough for this boy. He found it necessary to go "on beyond Z," or "on beyond Zebra." "In the places I go," he said, "there are things that I see that I never could spell if I stopped with the Z."

And do you know what? That's absolutely true in our relationship with God. Our little alphabet is completely inadequate when it comes to describing God, especially when it comes to describing what God has done for your and my salvation—and our neighbors'. Jesus says, simply and clearly, "All things are possible with God." This means God can do things in your neighbors' lives that are beyond description. In fact, God can do things that are "on beyond" our imagination—including things he can do for your neighbors through people like you and me (Ephesians 3:20).

"But you don't know my neighbor!" you might be saying. That's true. I don't know your neighbor. I don't know the pain he or she has had. I don't know how thick your neighbor's skin is against the work of the Holy Spirit. I don't know how skilled your neighbor is in tying your thoughts into knots when you try to share your faith with him. I don't know your neighbor and the unique challenge she is for you.

But I do know something about God. God can do the impossible. He saved you and me. He also has the desire to save your neighbor. These are miracles we can't begin to describe! And God is the one who does them!

Sometimes we need to be reminded that God doesn't expect us to do miracles. He simply wants us to pray for our neighbors, show them we care, and share his message of good news in Jesus. God wants us to live as examples of Jesus' love for our neighbors.

As we pray for our neighbors, God's Spirit works at preparing their hearts to receive him. As we pray, God's Spirit also works in us to give us the compassion and care for our neighbors that God himself has. And in the meantime God prepares opportunities for us to spend time with and talk with our neighbors. All we have to do is be faithful, listening, looking for needs to be filled, and sharing about how much God means to us. And in God's strength we can do that (Philippians 4:13)!

Let God work through you in surprising ways. God's love for you and your neighbor in his wonder-filled life for you goes "on beyond Zebra"!

Reflect/Act

How has God been "on beyond Zebra" in your life? Make a list of four or five ways in which God has been this way in our world and in your life.

Commit to praying earnestly for your neighbors this week, and if God presents you with opportunities, share your love for the Lord with your neighbors.

Prayer Starters for Praying Mark 10:24-27

- *Praise* God that his grace reaches all the way into your life, into your neighborhood, and into the lives of each person you will meet today.
- *Ask* God to fill you with a love that is "on beyond Zebra." Ask God to give you his love for your neighbor.
- *Thank* God that he is able to do the impossible. Thank God, too, for his desire to do the impossible in your life and in your neighbors' lives.

Pray a BLESSing on those who live or work near you:

- **Body.** Be courageous. Be daring. Ask God to bring bodily healing into the lives of your neighbors.

- **Labor.** Ask that something "on beyond Zebra" might happen in your neighbors' work on the job, at school, or at home.
- **Emotional.** Pray that your next-door neighbors, co-workers, or class-mates may sense a joy that causes them to wonder who its source is.
- **Social.** Ask God to bring quality friendships into your neighbor's lives. Pray that your relationships with them may grow.
- **Spiritual.** Pray that God's grace may overwhelm all the people in your life. "God so loved the world that he gave his one and only Son" for everyone who believes (John 3:16)! That's "on beyond Zebra"!

DAY 23

DEVELOPING A RELATIONSHIP

The Lord said to Cain, "Where is your brother Abel?"
"I don't know," he replied. "Am I my brother's keeper?"
—GENESIS 4:9-10

Yes, you are your brother's keeper. The essence of being a Christian is a relationship—a personal, one-on-one relationship with Jesus Christ. And Jesus calls us to "love one another"—even our enemies (John 13:34; Matthew 5:44-45). So being a Christian also involves relationships with all other human beings—for all are created in God's image (Genesis 1:26-27).

Relationship takes time. They take energy; they take commitment; they involve risk. Relationships can bring incredible blessings; they can also bring excruciating pain. God has experienced all of these in his relationship with each one of us.

The same can happen to you as you take the step of sharing the gospel—the good news of Jesus—with your neighbors. I'm not going to sugarcoat this one. If you want to involve yourself in one of the greatest experiences of the Christian life—realizing that the Spirit of Christ has used you in some significant way to make an impact on one of your neighbors for the Lord for eternity—it will cost you.

All relationships involve a healthy investment. In the next several days we're going to look at how you can begin to make such an investment. But before we start, it's critical that you place yourself in the hands of the God who promises to walk alongside you. Place yourself in the hands of the one who has already made the ultimate investment in your life and in the life of your neighbor.

It's important to know that your neighbor is a person of inestimable value. Your neighbor matters to God. Your neighbor is precious to Christ, who was willing to sacrifice his own life for him or her.

If that's how valuable your neighbor is to God, if he or she matters that much to God, then you and I need to make the commitment to treat that neighbor with love and sensitivity. If God loves your neighbor that much, then the time, the energy, the joy, and even the possible pain or discomfort of developing a relationship with that neighbor is a small price for you to pay.

Think about being a channel of God's love to your neighbor. Think about being an instrument God can use to reveal himself to your neighbor. Ask God today to help you pray for, care for, and share with your neighbor, entering into relationship for Jesus' sake.

God wants to do amazing things through you. Are you ready?

Reflect/Act

God uses a variety of ways to bring us into relationship with himself. Most often, though, he chooses to introduce himself through other human beings. Take some time to reflect on how God used people to introduce you to Christ. Who were those people?

What can you do to make yourself a more usable instrument through which Christ can reveal himself?

Prayer Starters for Praying Genesis 4:9-10

- *Praise* God for loving you as a person of inestimable value.
- *Thank* him for the people in your life who have considered you their brother or sister in the Lord.
- *Confess* to God any ways in which you have ignored the physical, emotional, and spiritual needs of people whom he considers to be your brothers and sisters. Ask God to forgive you for these shortcomings.
- *Ask* God to bring to your mind the name of anyone in your relational circle (family, neighborhood, classmates, co-workers) whom he desires to adopt into his family, as your spiritual brother or sister. When God brings names to your mind, write them down and begin praying for them.
- *Ask* God to help you view each of your neighbors as a person of inestimable value.

Pray a BLESSing on those who live or work near you:

- **Body.** Ask God to meet your neighbors' needs for health, strength, and safety from bodily harm.
- **Labor.** Pray that your neighbors may do their work well as a way of building on their relationship with the Lord.

- **Emotional.** Pray that the Lord will let your neighbors know how precious they are to him, and that they may experience his peace today.
- **Social.** Ask God to help your neighbors develop caring relationships with the people in their lives and to avoid any competitive rivalries at home, at school, or in the workplace.
- **Spiritual.** Pray that your neighbors may experience a growing awareness of God's presence in their lives, and that he loves them and calls them to serve him and others.

DAY 24

AWARE

O Lord, you have searched me and you know me. You know when I sit and when I rise; you perceive my thoughts from afar. You discern my going out and my lying down; you are familiar with all my ways.
—PSALM 139:1-3

As you begin to develop a relationship with your neighbor, there are three As that will help. God calls us to be Aware, Alert, and Accepting. We'll talk about each of these As in the next three days.

First, God calls us to be Aware. Always be aware that God loves your neighbor more than you do. God has provided for the needs of your neighbor from the riches of his eternal glory. God has a preferred future for your neighbor, filled with hope and promises. More than anything else, God wants a personal relationship with your neighbor that is every bit as intimate as the one he shares with you. God wants to give your neighbor his salvation to new life.

So as you begin to move toward the fantastic privilege of being used to introduce your neighbor to the Lord Jesus, never, ever forget that this is God's plan, God's hope, God's dream, God's desire for your neighbor. Be aware that you will play an important part in the process but that God is the one who will be saving your neighbor.

Here's an illustration that might help. Imagine God making his way down some superhighway toward your neighbor's life. Imagine yourself "merging" onto that highway and simply following the direction God has already set.

One of the things I need to remember every day of my life, and most often in my desire to be used to bring others to Christ, is that God works around the clock. Sometimes I wonder if God created us with a need to sleep so that we would be "out of the way" once in a while, so that he would be able to get some work done without our interference. Each morning, as you and I open our eyes, we need to check in with the Lord to find out just how far he has traveled down that highway while we've been sleeping. We need to be tuned in to God's working closer and closer to the heart of our neighbor's greatest need.

Celebrate the marvelous fact that God has invited you to be part of the greatest enterprise in his world: reconciliation—that is, restoring the relationships of men, women, and children in your neighborhood to the God who has created them and loves them!

Praise God this day for his amazing love and salvation! Praise him for his watchful care for you and your neighbors every minute of every day! Praise God for calling you to be part of his great work of renewing relationships with your neighbors!

Reflect/Act

God is absolutely aware of every detail of every life. Celebrate that fact today. Be aware that nothing is held secret from God.

Make a list of the things God has done to open the way for you and your neighbor to renew a right relationship with him. This list will heighten your awareness of just how much God has invested himself in our eternal salvation and life.

Prayer Starters for Praying Psalm 139:1-3
- *Thank* God for his knowledge of you and of everything about you.
- *Ask* God to give you the courage to evaluate and confess anything in your life that you aren't pleased to have him know about. Ask God for his forgiveness and help in putting things right in your life.
- *Thank* God for his commitment to you and your neighbor.
- *Ask* God to help you join him in his mission to adopt your neighbor into his family and to introduce your neighbor to the Savior.

Pray a BLESSing on those who live or work near you:
This is a good day to review the prayers you have been offering to God for your neighbor. Repeat your prayers from last week. Add some new ones as God increases your knowledge of your neighbor's life and needs.
- **Body.** Ask God to bless your neighbors with health, strength, and bodily healing today.
- **Labor.** Ask God to work miracles in your neighbors' workplaces or classrooms today and to help them see his hand working in their lives.
- **Emotional.** Pray that your neighbor, co-worker, or classmate may

experience the joy of God's presence and know his peace.

- **Social.** Ask God to bring quality friendships into your neighbors' lives, and to reveal himself to your neighbors through you and others. Pray that your relationships with your neighbors may grow.
- **Spiritual.** Pray that God's grace may overwhelm your neighbor or co-worker. Just think of it! God so loves the world that he gave his one and only Son to restore our relationship with him!

DAY 25

ALERT

"The eyes of the Lord are on the righteous and his ears are attentive to their prayer." —1 PETER 3:12

You may already have noticed that when you make the commitment to pray for your neighbor, the Holy Spirit develops the desire within you to care for your neighbor. When you make yourself available to God, he will take you up on your offer. So, please, for Jesus' sake and your neighbor's sake, be *alert*. Follow God's example. Keep your eyes and ears open, attentive, and ready to respond.

Relationships with your neighbors can be based on a variety of things. Be alert to how the Spirit may open doors for you to grow in your relationship with your neighbor.

Keep your eyes and ears open, not in an intrusive or nosy way, but in a way that reflects the concern of Jesus for each individual. Look for small and seemingly insignificant ways in which you can serve your neighbors. Don't make a big deal out of the things you do. Your neighbors may not even notice at first, but that doesn't matter. God notices.

For example, when you drag your trash barrel back up the driveway, maybe you could drag your neighbor's barrel up too. If a stray newspaper is caught in your neighbor's shrubbery, pick it up. Also be alert to ways in which the Holy Spirit will open up ways for you to engage in conversation and service.

Let me tell you about one of my red-letter experiences. Years ago I lived on the sixth floor of a high-rise apartment building in southeast Denver. My neighbor, Vera, was an elderly woman. During the four years that I was her neighbor, I never observed anyone coming to visit. Her life seemed to center around three outings a day—in the morning, in midafternoon, and late in the evening—when she would take a walk with her pet schnauzer, Otto. One day I realized that I had missed Vera and Otto. So I wrote a note that simply said, "I've missed you and Otto. Is everything okay?" and taped it to her apartment door. That evening, when I returned home, there was a note taped on my front door. It read,

"I didn't think anyone would notice. Otto is dead."

It didn't take a lot of intelligence for me to realize that my neighbor was suffering from a deflated self-image and grief. I took the elevator back downstairs, walked across the street to the bakery, and bought a half dozen cookies. I returned to Vera's front door and knocked. "How about making me some tea?" I asked. That night Vera and I shared tea and cookies. We also shared our stories, and she cried softly but deeply as she shared how much she missed Otto.

That conversation helped lead into a friendship between Vera and me. Vera isn't a Christian . . . yet. But throughout the years her Christmas cards have changed from those with little dogs wearing holiday bows to cards with a spiritual hint to them. And Vera keeps asking questions about my church and my relationship with Jesus. The Holy Spirit is working in Vera's life, and I know that someday she's going to take that critical step into her Lord's open arms.

Be alert to what's happening with your neighbors. When God opens a door, walk through it.

Reflect/Act

Spend some time thinking about how much peace you experience knowing that your loving and powerful God is always watching over you and is ready to listen to you.

Take a walk around your neighborhood. What do you see that tells you something about your neighbors and their needs?

Prayer Starters for Praying 1 Peter 3:12

- *Praise* God for the amazing truth that he is concerned about even the mundane and insignificant things that happen in our lives. Nothing we bring to him is too small for his attention and concern.
- *Thank* God that he has promised not only to listen but also to be thoughtfully attentive to all your prayers.
- *Ask* God to sharpen your spiritual sight and hearing to the needs and concerns of your neighbor.

Pray a BLESSing on those who live or work near you:

Be specific today. You've prayed for your neighbors for quite some time, and God has been softening your heart and intensifying your senses to be more and more alert to the special concerns that fill your neighbors' lives. What are they?

- **Body.** Pray today that your neighbors may be free of any frustrating illnesses or nagging physical discomforts.
- **Labor.** Pray that your neighbors' employment may provide opportunities for them to express themselves in creative, meaningful ways. Ask your neighbors how their work is going, and ask how you can pray for them in their everyday work.
- **Emotional.** Ask God to help you be alert to your neighbors' emotional health.
- **Social.** Pray that God will keep you alert to the opportunity simply to be your neighbors' friend.
- **Spiritual.** Pray that you will be alert to the questions your neighbors may have about God and about having a relationship with him.

DAY 26

ACCEPTING

"Come, see a man who told me everything I ever did. Could this be the Christ?" —JOHN 4:29

At the center of any good relationship is an *accepting* spirit. All of us have our funny little tendencies and flaws. All of us have rough edges. All of us have habits that can be irritating.

Your neighbors may not always be the easiest people to have a relationship with. They may be engaged in habits that offend you. They may have made choices that you would never have made. They may not live with the same values or follow the same rules. They may not discipline their children in a way you respect. Maybe they play their stereo at ear-breaking volumes. Maybe they use cooking spices that permeate the apartment complex. Or perhaps they are committed to a religious stance that is totally opposed to Jesus Christ. Worse yet, they may be completely hostile and openly judgmental of your life and your commitment to Christ.

Jesus accepts each of us exactly where we are. In his conversation with the woman at Jacob's well in our Scripture for today, he talked with her about her current relationship and her previous marriages. (See John 4:1-4.) He didn't condemn her on the spot. He treated her with respect as a human being. But having done that, Jesus also worked with her to bring her to a better place in life and into a life-changing relationship with him.

God's goal, and our goal with him, is to do whatever is possible to bring our neighbor into a personal relationship with Jesus as Savior and Lord. But, please, as you develop a relationship with your neighbor, do so with an accepting spirit. Accept your neighbors as human beings who, like yourself, have funny little tendencies and flaws, some rough edges, and some irritating habits. Beginning your relationship with words of judgment or corrections won't enhance the work of the Spirit in their lives or your involvement with them.

Once they come to know Christ, they will join you in submitting themselves to the Holy Spirit's transforming work in their lives. They will begin to become more and more like Jesus as the Spirit works in their hearts, making them pure and holy. Leave that work to the Spirit. Your responsibility is to provide them a safe, accepting, and nonjudgmental relationship. The greatest blessing you can bring into your neighbor's life is the blessing of acceptance and love—God's love.

Reflect/Act

In what ways are you a flawed person?

Can you think of any judgments you may have passed on your neighbors for things they have done or left undone?

What can you do to show an accepting spirit to your neighbors today?

Prayer Starters for Praying John 4:29

- *Praise* God, who is perfect, for his ability to accept us in love even "while we were still sinners" (Romans 5:8).
- *Thank* God for accepting you.
- *Celebrate* with God his ability to love the unlovable, accept the unacceptable, and forgive the sinner.
- *Ask* God to help you develop a more accepting spirit. Ask the Holy Spirit to grow in you the fruit of the Spirit, especially in your relationships with neighbors, classmates, co-workers, and others who may be different from you.

Pray a BLESSing on your neighbors, using Romans 5:6-11:

- Ask God today to help you be the reflection of his acceptance and love for your neighbor, knowing that Christ died for each one of us because we are "powerless" to save ourselves.
- Ask the Lord to help your neighbors see that "while we were still sinners, Christ died for us."
- Pray that the Holy Spirit will work in your neighbors' hearts, even as they are God's enemies, to reconcile them to God "through the death of his Son" and to save then "through his life." Also ask the Spirit to help you love these neighbors, even if they are acting as enemies toward you.
- Ask the Lord to move your neighbors to join with you as you "rejoice in God" for reconciliation (restored relationships) "we have now received" through Jesus Christ.
- Pray also for your neighbors' various daily needs, opening yourself to love and accept your neighbors with grace and truth.

DAY 27

DETERMINING A NEED

*Praise the Lord, O my soul; all my inmost being, praise his holy name.
Praise the Lord, O my soul, and forget not all his benefits—who
forgives all your sins and heals all your diseases, who redeems your
life from the pit and crowns you with love and compassion, who
satisfies your desires with good things so that your youth is renewed
like the eagle's.* —PSALM 103:1-5

W hen visiting my home last week, my nephew said, "I'm really hungry!"

Without too much thought, I knew that he had noticed the empty candy jar in the living room. He wanted some chocolate—his and my favorite.

I wonder how he would have responded if I had offered to get him some broccoli? That wouldn't have fed his "hunger." A hamburger probably wouldn't have done the trick either. Neither would a hot dog.

My nephew was looking for chocolate! His need wasn't really an empty stomach. His parents feed him regularly. No, his need was related to his "sweet tooth"—something I can strongly identify with.

When sharing about Jesus and his gospel message with your neighbor, it's very important for you to be sensitive to your neighbor's individual, specific need. If I had given my nephew some broccoli or a hamburger, I would have missed his real need.

Jesus comes very intimately, very sensitively into each of our lives. He meets us exactly where we are. He's available to meet each individual need.

As you continue developing a relationship with your neighbor, start asking yourself this question: "What area, what concern, what question in my new friend's life is most in need of the presence of Jesus?"

You don't have to go far to find a possible answer to that question. Answer it for yourself. You have more in common with your neighbor (even your unsaved neighbor) than you might care to admit. Your neighbor most likely has some financial concerns. Don't you? Your neighbor may not be feeling appreciated at work. Have you ever felt that way? One neighbor may be concerned about her youngest child. Another may be concerned about his oldest. Maybe you know what that's like.

Or perhaps your neighbors had a major scare last week when their doctor told them the results of a physical exam. Or maybe your neighbor lost her mother to cancer last fall. You know these things could happen to you, if they haven't already.

Your neighbor's needs are similar in many ways to your own. This week, ask the Spirit to help you be sensitive to what those needs are. Look for opportunities to help your neighbor in specific ways.

Reflect/Act

In what ways has God met your specific needs in his surprising, creative ways?

Don't forget God's benefits. In fact, make a list of them right now. Take note of how the Lord uniquely ministers to your individual needs.

What things do you hold in common with your neighbor? Are you both too busy? Are you both stressed over finances? Do you have a common concern for your children? Find out by talking with your neighbor this week.

Prayer Starters for Praying Psalm 103:1-5

- *Praise* God and thank him for all his benefits in your life.
- *Celebrate* God's creativity, thanking him for the way in which he takes into account our unique personalities as he reveals himself to us.
- *Thank* God that he loves all of us enough to meet us right where we are.
- *Ask* God to help you understand your neighbor's unique personality. Invite God to open your mind to the specific way in which your neighbor would be most open to hearing or seeing or experiencing the things of God.

Pray a BLESSing on those who live or work near you:

- **Body.** Pray that these neighbors may praise God today for his benefits of health, medicine, rest, and relaxation. Ask God to heal all your neighbors' diseases and to renew their strength.
- **Labor.** Ask God to help your neighbors appreciate the skills and abilities they have and to think about who blessed them with these gifts.

- **Emotional.** Pray that God may satisfy your neighbors' desires and emotional needs, as only he can.
- **Social.** Pray that your neighbors may enjoy the time they spend with friends, family, and anyone else today.
- **Spiritual.** Ask that your neighbors may confess all their sins and experience God's forgiveness, love, and compassion. Pray that they may know for certain that God has taken note of them.

DAY 28

BE INTERRUPTIBLE

I heard the voice of the Lord saying, "Whom shall I send? And who will go for us?" And I said, "Here am I. Send me!" He said, "Go . . ."
—ISAIAH 6:8-9

Of all the household chores, I hate ironing the most. I hate it so much that I have my shirts laundered.

April (not her real name) works early mornings at the cleaners. We're on a first-name basis. She knows I'm a pastor. I know she is single and cares for three elementary-school-age grandchildren. While it has been rather obvious to me that April likes to talk, she hasn't shared with me whether she's divorced or widowed, and I don't know the circumstances that led her to take in her grandchildren. Several months ago she asked if she could "confess" to me that she hadn't been to church since she was married, except for a handful of funeral services and an occasional Christmas and Easter service.

You need to know that last January 1, I put April on my "hit" list. I've been praying that God would use me in any way possible to share Christ with April.

Recently I stopped at the cleaners on my way to an early morning meeting. I was running late, but I thought that if I could just run in and out, I could make my meeting on time. It looked possible. There were no other cars in the parking lot. April was at the computer when I came in, so she immediately typed in my name, noting the four shirts I brought in and the "on hangers and heavy starch" instructions. As I was reaching for the door, I said, "Have a good day!"

April responded with a sober, "I will, physically."

I'm not the most sensitive person in the world, but even I recognized her words as a rather unique response. Within a fraction of a second the Holy Spirit reminded me that one stressed-out grandmother is of infinitely more value to God than any meeting. The Spirit sensitized me to the fact that I just might be on the threshold of an interruption that could turn into a holy moment. I decided to be obedient to the Spirit. I asked, "April, is there something wrong with the rest of you?"

With tears welling up in her eyes, April told me that she didn't think she could keep up with the pace of caring for her grandchildren. She just felt overwhelmed and alone. With a choking voice she asked, "Do you think God would be willing to come back into my life?"

Within the next two to three minutes I had the profound honor of being able to lead April in a prayer of recommitment to the Savior and Lord she had left decades earlier.

God loves to interrupt our lives—not in a negative way but in a way that surprises us with opportunities to join him in his mission here on earth. God's will is always done, regardless of our responsiveness. But don't miss the excitement of being interrupted from what you have planned. God wants you to join with him in fulfilling his plan.

Reflect/Act

Have you ever told God that he may interrupt you? God's plan will be accomplished through someone, but he isn't in the habit of drafting someone into service. He uses volunteers.

If God wanted to "send" you somewhere to someone, could he find room in your schedule?

Prayer Starters for Praying Isaiah 6:8-9

- *Praise* the Lord for his great plan of salvation and for his willingness to use us to help bring others to him.
- *Confess* any carelessness you may have shown by not listening to others' needs for spiritual comfort or for not being available to share Christ with others.
- *Ask* God to give you the willingness to be used by him. Like Isaiah, pray this prayer: "Here am I. Send me!"
- *Ask* God for the courage to be obedient when he takes you up on your offer.

Pray for your neighbors as your relationship with them develops:
Ask God to help you pray faithfully for the people on your prayer list. Review the BLESS prayer in connection with your neighbors. Continue to be more specific in your requests as your relationships with them grow. Pray also that if God chooses to "send" you to your neighbors, you will be

willing and interruptible. Ask for God's help in setting priorities so that you can be available. Ask for wisdom to speak God's message of love and salvation in a way that meets your neighbors' needs.

DAY 29

KNOW YOUR CONTEXT

Buy the truth and do not sell it; get wisdom, discipline and understanding. —Proverbs 23:23

I will never grow tired of watching the Holy Spirit at work. He uses such unique and curious ways to bring people to a relationship with Christ. That's why it's so important for us to commit to being able to use every opportunity to be witnesses for Jesus' sake.

The second thing we have to do is commit ourselves to know the context we are working in. Make yourself available to conversations with your neighbors about a whole variety of subjects. Most of your neighbors will need to be comfortable in talking with you about common, everyday things before they'll be comfortable in talking about their spirituality. Don't ignore what might be important or interesting to your neighbor.

How can you be ready to talk about a variety of subjects? Be aware of what's happening in the international political scene. Know which movies are drawing the crowds in your hometown. Know the titles on the best-seller book lists. If your neighbor has a dog, do you know what breed it is? If your neighbor gardens, have you asked to take a closer look? Do you know which schools or colleges your neighbor's children attend? Ask about their holiday traditions. Ask about their unique professional challenges. Ask about their favorite foods.

The Holy Spirit can use any one of these topics as an entrance point for you to begin a conversation that can help you develop a relationship with your neighbor. And as you develop a relationship, you'll begin to know your neighbor's heart, and your neighbor will begin to know yours.

Let me tell you about one such experience. Several years ago, I was privileged to be part of a new church-planting ministry. Early in that project, the members of the core group went door to door, interviewing neighbors to find out the needs of the families in the area around our new building site. We expected that one point of contact would be time management or the setting of priorities. We anticipated holding Christian perspective seminars on those important topics and inviting our unchurched or misbelieving neighbors as our guests.

But do you know what the number one need in our new and fast-growing neighborhood turned out to be? Potty training! That's right. These upwardly mobile, extremely busy, work-addicted "busters" perceived that their number one "crisis" was in knowing how to best help their young children (and there were thousands in that community) outgrow their need for diapers. So we responded by hosting a "Potty Training" seminar, to which we invited a pediatrician, a child psychologist, and our neighbors.

And do you know what? As a result of the relationships that gradually developed between church members and the one hundred neighbors who met at that three-hour seminar, ten persons eventually came to know Jesus as the Lord of their lives.

Know your neighbors. Know what's important to them. Be able to have intelligent conversations with them about the things they value. As followers of Christ, we need to "earn" the right to speak to the most important, eternal needs of our neighbors. Start to earn that right by knowing the context of their everyday lives.

Reflect/Act

How have your prayers increased your desire to know your neighbors in a caring way?

What have you learned about your neighbors? Commit to learning more about them so that you can relate to them in a way that shows God's love for them and leads to sharing the good news of Christ.

Prayer Starters for Praying Proverbs 23:23

- *Praise* God for being the most intelligent, brilliant being in the universe! Our God knows everything!
- *Thank* God for his offer to give us wisdom when we ask for it (James 1:5).
- *Ask* God to "wise you up" regarding what's going on in our world. Do that for two reasons—so you can pray in a more informed way, and so you can increase the possible "connections" between you and your neighbors.

Pray a BLESSing for your neighbors, using ideas from 1 Corinthians 2:6-16:

- Pray that the Holy Spirit will protect your neighbors from the "wisdom of this age" so that they may understand "God's secret wisdom" revealed by his Spirit.

- Pray that your neighbors, with all the data available to them in this "information age," will not be distracted from the message of "what God has prepared for those who love him"—that is life and peace in the Lord's Presence forever, through Jesus Christ.

- Ask the Holy Spirit, who "searches all things," to help you understand what your neighbors' needs are.

- Pray that your neighbors, in the context of so much spiritual searching in our culture, may find Jesus Christ as the one, true way to the Father.

- Pray that both you and your neighbors may "have the mind of Christ."

DAY 30

KEEP ON PRAYING AND CARING

"All authority in heaven and on earth has been given to me. Therefore go and make disciples of all nations, baptizing them in the name of the Father and of the Son and of the Holy Spirit, and teaching them to obey everything I have commanded you. And surely I am with you always, to the very end of the age." —MATTHEW 28:18-20

As you finish this set of devotional readings, please remind yourself of two foundational truths: you have to keep on praying, and you have to keep on caring. Otherwise God won't be able to use you to keep on sharing. Without praying and caring, your sharing will be ineffective and will sound only like so many words.

The first important thing you can do for your neighbor is pray. Only in a vulnerable, honest, consistent relationship with God will you be able to follow the Spirit's leading in the next move you can make in your neighbor's life. Some of us have a tendency to rush into a relationship too fast. Others of us are far too restrained and silent to develop relationships in which people feel they can be open and vulnerable. Only in prayer will God provide you with the leading from the Spirit that you will need to know you are moving along in his power.

Be sure, too, always to ask for the Spirit's gifts. He promises to give you the words to speak. He's already been working in your neighbor's heart. The Spirit has brought other people and other experiences into your neighbor's life. The one certain way to guarantee that you are the most usable communicator of God's Word to your neighbor is that you are consistently, daily connecting with God in prayer. And, remember, Jesus himself promises to be "with you always"!

The second important thing you can do for your neighbor is to keep on caring. Care for your neighbor in a sensitive, consistent way. Be aware of how much privacy your neighbor needs. Be aware of how your assertiveness may affect him or her. Be as Christ in his or her life. Your attitude, your kindness, your faithfulness as a friend can speak volumes.

And if you need a role model, look to Christ. He loves you and your neighbor and our entire world so much that he left heaven and became one of us. As one of us, he perfectly obeyed the Father, becoming the perfect sacrifice for our sins. That's how much Christ cares!

In the early days of church, believers in Christ were known for the way they always prayed for and loved each other. It's a poignant witness to the love of Christ. (See John 13:34-35.) It's the way God calls us to live so that his good news in Jesus can take root in people's lives and keep spreading to "all nations."

Reflect/Act

What will it take for praying, caring, and sharing to become a permanent lifestyle for you? Think back on all the things you've read in this book. Commit to making this lifestyle your lifestyle, for Jesus' sake. Ask for the Spirit's help. He wants to work miracles in you and through you.

Prayer Starters for Praying Matthew 28:18-20

- *Ask* God to help you bear in mind the essential task of the church and of every Christ-follower. We are called to be witnesses to the gospel of our Lord!
- *Thank* God for inviting you to join him in his work in this world.
- *Ask* God to use you and continue to use you in praying for your neighbors, caring for them, and sharing the good news of Christ's love with them, for Jesus' sake.
- *Ask* God for the salvation of your neighbor—and the next one, and the next one!

Pray BLESSings for those who live or work near you:

It cannot be said enough. If you and I, as children of the heavenly Father, keep asking for his Holy Spirit's work in the lives of our misbelieving friends, family members, co-workers, classmates, and others, what will happen to the kingdom of our great God? It will grow!

- Pray for "every good and perfect gift" from God, who "chose to give us birth through the word of truth" (James 1:17-18). God's desire is the salvation of the world—and that includes your neighbors.
- Pray for God's blessings on your neighbors—it's something you can be sure God wants—along with having you work alongside him in his great plan of salvation.

*Prayer*CONNECT

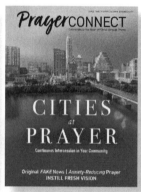
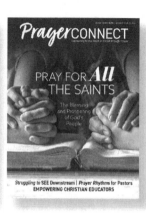

A NEW QUARTERLY MAGAZINE DESIGNED TO:

Mobilize believers to pray God's purposes for their church, city and nation.

Connect intercessors with the growing worldwide prayer movement.

Equip prayer leaders and pastors with tools to disciple their congregations.

Each issue of *Prayer Connect* includes:

- Practical articles to equip and inspire your prayer life.
- Helpful prayer tips and proven ideas.
- News of prayer movements around the world.
- Theme articles exploring important prayer topics.
- Connections to prayer resources available online.

Print subscription: $24.99
(includes digital version)

Digital subscription: $19.99

Church Prayer Leaders Network membership: $35.99 (includes print, digital, and CPLN membership benefits)